Creating A Good Social Order
Through Action Research

Creating a Good Social Order Through Action Research

Jean McNiff

with

Jack Whitehead & Moira Laidlaw and
Members of the Bath Action Research Group

with a foreword by John Field,
Director of Continuing Education,
University of Bradford

Hyde Publications

First edition 1992

Published by
HYDE PUBLICATIONS
3, Wills Road,
Branksome,
Poole, Dorset. BH12 1NQ

Typeset and Printed by Bourne Press,
3-11 Spring Road,
Bournemouth

ISBN 1 874154 00 7

Contents

*. . . faith by itself, if it is not
accompanied by action, is dead . . .
Therefore, prepare your minds for action;
be self-controlled; set your hope fully
on the grace to be given you when
Jesus Christ is revealed.*

James, 2:17; 1 Peter 1:13

Acknowledgements

This book represents a collaborative enterprise.

I thank all the action researchers with whom I have worked, for teaching me so much.

I especially need to thank the members of the Bath action research group for their help and encouragement.

John Field, Director of Continuing Education at the University of Bradford, has given his time and support generously, and I thank him for that.

Moira Laidlaw and Jack Whitehead made it all possible, and for this I am grateful.

Thank you to Alan Hyde, my husband, for making it all come right.

Participants in the conversations:

RON ADAMS
PHIL COATES
KEVIN EAMES
MARY GURNEY
TERRY HEWITT
ERICA HOLLEY
MOIRA LAIDLAW
PETER MELLETT
JACK WHITEHEAD

Foreword

Action research is about learning. It involves us in active, open-ended and vigorous reflection upon our work and its consequences. Doing action research requires us to draw upon our own resources, individual and mutual, as experienced practitioners. It is an attractive process because it has to do not only with the production of knowledge for its own sake (though it has a contribution to make in that respect), nor with identifying technical improvements in our job (though it can help us understand the preconditions of "good practice"); it also has to do with emancipation.

At the core of Jean McNiff's book is the belief that professional development is closely bound up with personal development; and that both processes can be fostered by a dialogue of equals. As a text, the book embodies the kinds of practice which it discusses: it intermingles debate with analysis in a way that raises as many questions, and in as fruitful a way, as the substance. As a result, we have a text which takes quite a few risks, in a way which seems to me highly congruent with the underlying principles of action research, and which stretches our understanding of ourselves as (striving to be) reflective practitioners.

I read this book in draft as someone who had only the haziest idea of what the University of Bath group is about. In its form and substance, the book led me to reflect and question in the way that you often hope for from open learning resources—and all too rarely get! Jean McNiff's approach is to emphasise the open-ended and diverse nature of action research as a process carried out by real human agents. There is, she says, no such thing as Action Research but there are action researchers. And the more action researchers in any society, one is tempted to add, the healthier it is likely to be. Phrases like "the learning society" tend to be thrown around at conferences and seminars without too much thought; "the learning society" (like the "learning company" or even "learning school") is plainly a Good Thing. This book describes one small, and probably transient, learning community; we need more of them.

John Field, University of Bradford

Introduction

This book is the third in a series that explores the idea of personal and professional development through action research. The first in the series, 'Action Research: Principles and Practice' (Macmillan Education, 1988), is an introductory guide to action research—what it is, how it started, how and where it is being done, and so on. The main message in that book is that research should not be something that is done by professional educators on teachers, but should be something that teachers do as part of their everyday work. Some of these issues are summarised in Chapter 3. The second book, 'Teaching as Learning: an Action Research Approach' (Routledge, 1992), suggests that people develop as reflective practitioners through critiquing their own work, and offering their personal accounts for public criticism. In particular that book focuses on the problem of educational knowledge: who is a knower, and what is known, in terms of educational development—in short, what counts as educational knowledge. Some of these issues are summarised here in Chapter 2.

This present book explores the ideas of professional development being grounded in personal development, and how personal development is accelerated through critical reflection. It also develops the idea of how understanding is an aspect of human consciousness that has the potential for infinite development, and how dialogue, itself an evolutionary process, may enhance the growth of personal and collective understanding.

I am hoping to demonstrate the systematic form of my enquiry through the organisation of the text. One theme in my enquiry is the need to make public and share the values that guide our lives, through the way that we conduct our lives. I am applying that philosophy to the writing of this text. I feel it is important for us to live out our values and not simply to talk about them. I hope to show that process of values in action here in this book, by showing how the understanding of myself and others develops through conversations that are recorded in the text.

The presentation of this text is bound to be innovative. To some it might appear odd. To others it could have an appeal that will suggest that they might see things in a different light.

Content of the book

This book may be seen as my response to some perceived problematic issues within the action research movement. These issues need to be addressed by me as part of moving my own thinking forward, and by the education community in order for its current thinking to progress. For I perceive a certain stasis in the action research movement, a certain rigidity of thinking that is grounded within what is emerging for me as the paradox of action research. It is generally acknowledged in the literature that action research is an emancipatory enterprise whereby practitioners may feel free to follow through their own enquiry in whichever way seems most appropriate to the situation, provided they can demonstrate the scientific rigour which qualifies their enquiry as educational (Winter, 1989). However, within the very notions of 'emancipatory action research' and 'scientific rigour' there lurks the danger of prescription; that practitioners could be led to feel they are being advised to 'do such and such' in order to improve their practice. It is this form of advice that gives rise to the paradox. It is the same sort of paradox that I have to face in my life as an educator: how can I encourage people to be free in a non-coercive manner; encourage them actively to challenge what I, their teacher, have to say? How can I communicate to my companions the values which underpin my way of life without imposing those values on them? What form of self-reflective critique may I develop?

It is this sort of issue that constitutes the main focus of the work of a particular community of educational researchers that centre on the University of Bath. Individually and collectively we are offering a response to these issues, by demonstrating through the reality of our own lives, and the documents that are the 'linguistic photographs' of those lives, how and why we are attempting to realise our values in and through our work. As a member of that community I am offering this text as a photograph of that aspect of my life that is trying to overcome the paradox. I do not want to offer the text simply as another piece of theory to add to the literature. I want to demonstrate the practicality of educational enquiry as a generative transformational process.

What I want to do in this text is explore several basic substantial themes:

— the idea of action research as a critical form; not a *thing* so much as a *metaphor*;
— the idea of personal and professional development as the transformation of this critical form; not a sequential 'add on' process of collectable qualifications so much as a transformation of practice through developing insights;
— the idea of the transformation of practice through dialogue.

At a practical level, I may state these themes in terms of what I hope to encourage people to consider:

— that the educational community needs to look at action research as a way of looking at things, rather than a methodology to be applied;
— that managers within the professions need to accept the responsibility for the continuing personal and professional education of their practitioners;
— that the way to help people develop is to allow them to talk about themselves, and to take their own ideas as their guide to action; and that the facilitators of those dialogues should themselves be participants in the dialogues.

Form of the book

The book has two parts, both of which are located within the general procedure of an on-going enquiry. Part One operates from two perspectives, and constitutes two separate but interrelated texts. The outer text is constituted by conversations with two colleagues, Moira Laidlaw and Jack Whitehead. The conversations took place over a period of time, and focused originally as criticism of the various drafts of the inner text, giving rise to a 'book within a book' format. What is significant about this arrangement, however, is that the original 'inner' text arose in the first place out of conversations with these and other colleagues, and, in turn, the conversations recorded here arose out of the text. Subsequently a new text—the whole book—arose out of the conversations: and I have no doubt that many new conversations will be generated by the whole book. I hope that I am demonstrating the process of how practice may be transformed through dialogue; the idea that my practice is bound to and enfolded within yours, and yours in mine. I make the point within the inner text that dialogue is a way to improve ourselves, and I hope that the theory expressed within the inner text is picked up in the more practically-oriented outer one.

The inner text is a set of propositions— a report of my own present best thinking as to how we might tackle some of the critical issues facing the action research movement today; the outer text is a living example of how we do tackle them.

The theme of transforming practice is extended in Part Two in another set of conversations. This is a discussion with colleagues associated with the University of Bath who are sympathetic towards, yet critical of my own views. We discuss how, through our sense of community, we can (1) express our practical intention about improving our work in the name of education and our own humanity, in a dialogical form, in a way which will enable our group to judge our own and each other's effectiveness; (2) how the production of this text can embody a developing critical understanding of our educational development in our enquiries of the form 'How do I improve ... ?' (Whitehead, 1989a and b). In this section I explain my own ideas about the generative transformational nature of action research as a form of educational theory, and I attempt to show the interplay between the theory and the practice through the content and the arrangement of the text.

I like the conversation between David Bohm and F. David Peat (Bohm and Peat, 1987), as they remember how they began collaborating professionally:

David Peat: ... After I returned to Canada, it was clear that we should go on meeting again on a fairly regular basis to continue our dialogues.

David Bohm: Yes, but it also began to emerge that the dialogue itself was the key issue. And that this was intimately related to all the others. The essential question was: How can we engage in dialogue in a creative way?

David Peat: Yes, and I think this was what eventually led me to suggest that we should write a book together. In a sense, working on this book has become a continuation of our dialogue. Of course, many of the ideas we're going into really began with you.

David Bohm: Yes, but in exploring them through dialogue they began to develop in new ways and it also became possible to communicate them more clearly.

David Peat: Communication plays a very important role in how new ideas can develop.

For my part, I hope this book, both in form and in substance, may be seen as part of the process of communication between the participants who contributed to the dialogues encapsulated herein, and between the participants in the wider community who will want to sustain the dialogue.

Audience

In these terms, then, I have no one audience in mind other than practitioners in all walks of life who share a common sense of purpose that they want to reflect critically upon what they are doing with a view to improving it, and sharing that process with others—action researchers. I make the point throughout that my own work is in teaching, and that most progress in action research has been done within the teaching profession. This model, however, may generalise to other workplaces.

I would like to think, also, that this book is sustaining the view I began developing some years ago, that books do not exist only as artefacts within the lives of the people who read them. They are the synthesising of the present best thinking of the author(s); but it must readily be acknowledged by the writer and the reader (the participants in the discourse) that this is a form of active discourse in which the intention is to deconstruct what is presented with a view to reconstruction in a better form (see Chapter 3).

This book is not only pages between covers. It is the story of the transforming lives of its creators, and, as such, is an active aspect of their development (see also McNiff, 1991). The creators have in fact moved on beyond the book. It is their legacy, the shadow-skin that they shed as they moved on in their thinking because of the thinking-together that constitutes the book. But the book remains to be shared now with others, to show the process whereby the creators came to leave it behind.

Such is the nature of discourse. Such is the nature of action research.

Action research: an overview

Let me begin with a brief rationale for action research to locate the discussion, and then point out some of the critical issues that are current in the movement.

Action research is the name given to a kind of research that has become increasingly popular, particularly in Britain, as a way in which practitioners evaluate their own work. It has been developed mainly in the field of education as a coherent approach to the professional learning of teachers; but it is being used more and more in professional development schemes within other fields. In many ways, education as a profession has provided a lead for workers in other walks of life to follow; some current action research models are being applied within professional development schemes—for example, for nurses, police, and management trainers and consultants.

What makes action research distinctive is that it is done by practitioners themselves, instead of, as in traditional forms of research, a professional researcher doing research on practitioners. The research is carried out by the practitioner because she wants to improve her own work, and the research programme begins with her identification of a particular aspect of her work, here and now, that she wants to investigate.

The way that action research operates is through a problem-solving approach. It follows through an action plan of identification of problem—proposed solution—implementing the solution—evaluation of the solution—modification of practice. The practitioner tries out different ways of doing things, reflects on what she has done, and, in the light of her reflections, tries out a new way. This process has come to be known generally as action-reflection, though there is no single standard term used in the literature. The process is cyclical, in that a modified new form of practice itself holds aspects that need attention. Each time we go through such a cycle, it is called by most researchers an action-reflection cycle. It is not difficult to see that this process is on-going: as soon as we reach a tentative solution to an identified problem, the solution itself may become problematic, and we begin another new cycle. This process has given rise to a 'cycle of cycles' conceptualisation, or, in some visualisations, a 'spiral of spirals' (see McNiff, 1988).

The action research movement arose in the late 1960s and early 1970s, mainly as a reaction to the then dominant disciplines approach to professional education, particularly as it was promoted within teacher education. This approach held that it is possible to study the constituent parts of a professional field, and apply that study to one's own practice in order to improve it. In initial and in-service teacher education, teachers were required to study the philosophy, psychology, history and sociology (and, later, management) of education, and apply what they had learnt to their work in education. This approach was theory-driven: that is, a generalised theory was taken as the starting point for a programme of professional development. Teachers fitted their practice to a given theory. Success was judged in terms of how well teachers' practices matched the guidelines that the theory proposed.

Action research developed as a form of practical research which legitimated teachers' attempts to understand their own work from their own point of view. Instead of following the disciplines, and applying the theory to themselves, they were encouraged to explore what they were already doing and propose ways of improving it, thus drawing their own personal theories out of their practice (Whitehead, 1983). In this way the practical wisdom of teachers is enhanced, as is their status as self-reflective professionals.

The movement was given focus by several prominent individuals, notably Lawrence Stenhouse and John Elliott of the University of East Anglia; Stephen Kemmis, also of UEA but now at Deakin University, Australia; and Jack Whitehead of the University of Bath. Their work has been instrumental in changing the face of educational theory and practice in Britain and the world, in at least three senses.

First, they have had profound impact on the daily lives of teachers, in that they have promoted a view of teachers as highly responsible individuals who are able personally to evaluate their work and improve it. Second, they have brought about a revolution in the notion of research. Research is no longer only something that is done by a professional researcher on a practitioner. It is a form of practice that intensely involves the personal commitment of the practitioner herself, whatever role or status she holds. As a result of this commitment by the practitioner to improve her work, that work itself becomes a form of research, in which she is constantly striving to improve. Research is not an 'add on', something to be done after work. It is the work itself.

Third, because of this scenario, educational theory is being re-defined, particularly in the work of Jack Whitehead and his notion of a 'living educational theory'. Whereas theory was once grounded in the disciplines of education, now it is grounded in the real lives of teachers as they try to do what is best for themselves and for the people in their care.

As indicated above, I feel that the action research movement is now having to tackle some basic issues. The way it deals with them will determine its future direction. Much is written currently about action research as an instrument for social and cultural change, and the critical issues are identified as social, economic, political and cultural (for example, Day, 1991). My own view (see also Bloom, 1987) is that this is not a social crisis, so much as an intellectual one. The crisis that action research is facing as an instrument of social change is grounded in the intellectual crisis of what constitutes legitimate educational knowledge.

This is a fundamental issue in this book. My own view is that there is too much emphasis placed on empiric approaches to forms of professional enquiry and professional development. I think this is one of the ways in which action research is not realising its full potential; for there is an insidious undercurrent that sees action research as a method to be applied. Indeed, this book could be interpreted in this light: here am I, telling you how to do action research. This is the last intention. This is not a 'how to do' book. There are already some very good ones on the market (e.g. Kemmis and McTaggart, 1982). This book offers a critical overview of some of the ways in which I, and others, are thinking about action research. Progressive new questions about the nature and appropriateness of action research are constantly emerging. I want to tackle some of these questions, and I suggest that, unless some of these issues are resolved, action research is in danger of becoming just another method that people can apply to practice, rather than a way of living that will improve practice.

I must stress a fundamental point, that, in my view, there is no 'correct' way of doing action research. Nor is there a 'true definition' of action research (I shall look at these issues in Chapter 1). The term 'action research' characterises a way of looking at things, an attitude, a way of thinking about thinking. This way in fact liberates people from believing that they have to look at things in any one particular way.

In this respect, this book does not set out to provide answers as to how you should conduct your personal and professional life; it does not aim to provide substantive guidance. It is here to explain what is going on in current thinking in action research as it is presented within the public domain, to point to emergent trends within the movement, and to suggest new directions.

Prologue

Here I am again, on the road to Bath.

I never tire of this journey. Banks of white blossom trees in May, like whipped cream heaped upon heavy hills; cascades of golden rain as Autumn winds whip the leaves smartly across flaring skies: I travel the long ribbons of road over the rolling Wiltshire downs and through the leafy valleys of Avon. Ten years I have been here and I never tire.

I first came here as a research student. I am now a Visiting Fellow. I work on a part-time distance basis, supporting teachers in the South of England in their studies for Higher Degrees. I also liaise with the action research group which meets in and around Bath.

I am working on a new text, exploring the idea of how personal and professional development may be strengthened through dialogue. I need to consult my colleagues in order to refine my own ideas; and show the reality of that process of refinement in and through the text, in order to show how I am living out my beliefs in my work.

I arrive. I love this place: a great monolith, chunks of concrete cubes hanging in frozen suspension over the lake.

Past the library, across the windswept first level. A bearded young man in carefully torn jeans opens the heavy door for me. Up the lattice stairs.

Jack's booming laughter gusts towards me as I pull open the swing doors. I'm here. They both rise to greet me.

Contact.

———————————

Jean   Let's talk about the text.

Jack   I feel worried that you were going over old ground. I feel here that you are refining the power of communicating ideas which you have already formulated through other texts. In those texts that I've read, I've always felt that there was a significant move forward, but in this text I haven't so far got that feeling. That creative move that I've always sensed in your other texts, I didn't yet feel was in there.

Jean   Do you mean in terms of substantial concepts? One of the purposes of writing this text was to present an overview of what is going on in thinking about action research.

Jack   Right. Now, it does that. This overview is written in the sense of an academic producing an overview. I was at a conference last week, and I felt very strongly something that you've been picking up for a long time, that people at other institutions and we at Bath seem to be thinking in different ways in relation to the creation of a living educational theory. Their focus seems to be the application of a particular social science in a policy arena, whereas ours seems to be an interest in the nature of educational theory. That's why I feel we need to concentrate on offering a redefinition of educational theory. I feel that in some way we need to adopt a strategy of focusing upon the ideas that we are generating here, and putting those up now as centrally important. In that way we would encourage a more active collaborative activity: subject our ideas to criticism and therefore move forward, and encourage others to do the same.

Jean   Where do you think the problem lies?

Jack   I felt very strongly last week that people were unwilling to engage with us. I felt quite a strong retrenchment going on in relation to what I can call 'older forms of thought', and I felt, maybe unjustly, an unwillingness to engage with the ideas about a living educational theory. Perhaps that's because people generally feel the need for the relative security of conceptual forms of thought, as I've said in my reply to Ortrun Zuber-Skerritt [page 52: JM]. Engaging in living forms of educational theory means risk. In your other texts, you've moved forward. In this one I think you have refined and offered a blueprint of a particular kind, which is of the same logical form to the one that traditionalist academics would offer—whereas what you have done in the past is always locate what you've produced in what you saw as a social need. So there you've produced something which will help us and others to move forward both practically and theoretically. I feel that this text doesn't take account of where we have moved since you produced the texts in 1987/88, in that we have now got a lot of people interested in the work on the ground in practice. But we have yet to offer a text of the kind which related to the idea that you had more than six months ago, about trying to publish the accounts of others, rather as you've done in the 1988 book, but which have more rigour. We have moved on in the quality of the accounts, and this fact is reflected in your overview. Perhaps we should be trying to integrate some of the ideas from the overview in a way that they might now practically show how they might be used by others in taking contexts forward within whole schools, with LEAs, with the General Teaching Council. It was that feeling that I had as I read it—I may be wrong in saying that I wanted more.

Jean   I too felt that need. The text seemed to be written almost in a propositional form. I wanted to say, 'Well, where's the evidence to back this up?'

Jean   The form of the book (as I saw it until a moment ago!) was that it would be arranged in two parts. Part One would be in that propositional form—my own thinking, my conceptualisation of current trends in action research. The conversation that we are actually having right now would constitute the first part of Part Two, which would then show the living reality of what I've said in Part One. The second bit of Part Two would be the conversation we're going to have with the others on 23rd November. Do you think that will work, or do you think that will be false? What I feel that we're actually doing here now is going through that action research cycle, but that is going to be very difficult to capture in a text, where we can show that development of thought. I fully accept what you're saying. I had hoped that the text would go through on that format—Part One, MY thinking, Part Two, OUR thinking, our critique on the book. However, what you're saying to me now is that, as you read Part One, it doesn't speak to you. You haven't got the evidence. Are we saying that I now need to re-write history and to build in the evidence as we go, because that in itself would be false in presenting the book.

Moira   I understand that.

Jean   How can we overcome the problem?

Jack   Perhaps if we looked at the ways we are intending to try to move forward over the next year or two, and then out of that set of intentions we might try to evaluate the effectiveness of what we're doing. It might then be possible to go back to the text and see if we've fulfilled our intentions. Yours would be related to this kind of text; ours would be related to the actual work that we're trying to do here.

Jean   There is another way forward, that we could transcribe this conversation that we're having now and put that in as a preface. We could put more conversations through the book, as the chapters progress, to give that sort of evidential support that you're talking about, make the point that in complying with the need that was expressed in the conversation that constitutes the preface, we've now built in the evidence. That would be our statement of intent, and the evidence of how we are trying to live out our stated intent. So this conversation, although conversation by its nature is linear, is in fact expressing the holistic view of our own lives. The conversation that we're having now is our practice, our developing practice, which has been generated out of some stimulus material (the text), while the stimulus material itself has been generated out of the practice. Would that make sense?

Jack   I think it would.

Moira   Yes, indeed. There's an integrity in that.

Jean   Yes, the text itself would take on its own integrity, and that would then reflect the conscious intent of its creators to show it as a living part of their lives; so that it is not what I said before, rewriting history; it's not playing false with history. It's aiming to demonstrate that holistic quality that we're trying to let shine through in our lives, in our doings with others. We are at liberty to go back into our own history and draw out the ideas that were latent then and are now taking explicit form. I like that!

Moira   So do I.

Jack   It also enables someone like myself to retain a view of their own individual integrity in what you've just said, the capacity to reflect back into one's own history, and see what was actually latent and now project it to a future form. But the recognition also that it is being done collaboratively within a community and is part of that community's development, so I think that should then enable someone like myself to hold both the one and the many at the same time.

Jean   I love that idea of Maslow's that each moment has its own history within itself and its own future dynamic within itself. I've always loved that idea of the now. It's the now that holds the past and the future.

Moira   Exactly. I think I do hold the idea that the experiences that we are involved in are always the past, the present and the future. Torbert has that in his 1991 text, that we have to keep a sense of what is past as well as a sense of what is going to be, because that's part of what is now.

Jack   I wonder, when I talk about something living and then the idea of the notion of a living theory, it's those three ideas that are central to it, that you understand present practice only as evaluation of the past with a future intention.

Jean   Do you think that would come across, if we interwove it into the text?

Jack   Yes. We've got the meeting soon with the action research group, where we should hopefully be able to project a number of other initiatives which we feel we could take over the next twelve months, two years. It seems to me that that would give us that notion of the future intention of a community, which we've never done before. For example, I've put down a set of criteria that I would like to be used to judge my effectiveness.

Jean   So, in terms of the structure of this book, what we could have would be some aspect of the conversation that we're having right now, a preface to locate the text, to locate the idea that we are trying to put forward a particular view of a living educational theory through the text. So we have the propositional bit where I'm explaining what I see as current trends in action research in the United Kingdom. I then need to build in that living evidence of how these ideas are being acted out in other people's lives. We can also build in the conversations that we'll have on 23rd November which will point to the future intent of other people within the community. In this way, the book itself would become the living reality of our community which would fulfil my purpose—and I do feel this quite strongly, as you were saying before. I perceive quite a strong division between the sort of logic that is being developed here and the forms of thinking that go on in other places. I simply felt this intuitively for a number of years and am perhaps becoming more aware, since I've become more public, I'm aware that there's quite a contradiction in the different ways of thinking about action research and the presentation of case studies.

Jack   You're right. I really have got to the point, which I haven't been at before, of saying that I think we need to get out into the public arena the sort of commitments we have, and try to describe and explain our own educational development as learners as an expression of 'How do I improve my practice in trying to make a better world for myself and others?'. I think we ought now to do that. The strategy that I have been adopting of expecting others to respond I think is no longer adequate. It's no longer adequate because others don't feel the need to engage in discussion about the nature of educational theory. I think it's now up to us.

University of Bath, 8th November, 1991

PART ONE

THE KNOWLEDGE BASE
OF EDUCATIONAL THEORY

Chapter One

What is the Nature of Action Research?

Moira   I like your comment about 'There's no such thing as action research—only action researchers'. Once you start trying to analyse action research, it is somewhere else. Once you try and actually pin down what it is, it's almost as if you've overshot, or you've not quite reached far enough. It's in the doing of something—it's in the trying to understand your own practice and improving it for the benefit of your own self improvement and the people with whom you're working that you actually understand what action research is. It's not in trying to understand the theory of what action research is.

Jean   I feel this strongly. It's something I've tried to articulate simply by writing it; and there's an example of the concept, perhaps, that we're trying to explore here. When I have an idea, the most efficient way I can find to try to capture the essence of that idea actually is to write about it. Now, for me, the writing itself is a vehicle whereby I can externalise what I feel intuitively. But if you were to ask me to try and characterise the thing itself, I don't think I would be able to do it, because this is inherent in the process. The process itself is the thing that I'm trying to understand. It's this process where I come to make explicit what I feel implicitly. Perhaps it is implicit simply because we cannot characterise it in a normative sense, in the common language that we all use—to try to make sense of our public lives. Possibly because it is essentially such a private thing, that it's part of our underlying competence that shapes the way we're going by trying to understand this driving force. In recent months I've come more and more to think of it in terms of spirituality—what's inside—I'm trying to understand that driving force. I think it's the sharing of the understanding that gives explicit form to the way we live our life. So I empathise very strongly with what you're saying, because this elusiveness of the values that underpin our lives is part of the exploration of living your own life, part of the excitement of being a thinking person.

Jack   I'd like to explore that idea of spirituality. I get to a point where I think there are certain qualities that are almost beyond the kind of comprehension that we can reach through our language, or our reflection, or our analysis. When you talk about spirituality, the word for me is 'ineffable'. I cannot get closer than affirming when I am with people when that quality is present. Even if I start to talk about it I lose it.

Moira   Yes, I know what you mean.

Jack   The closest I've ever got to it is in the poetic work of Martin Buber, 'I and Thou', when he talks about the 'I-You' relationship—not in relation to a God, but in relation to another human being. The only thing, if you like, that I feel as a value in life ultimately is in loving relationships and productive work. It's those two ideas of Fromm. So I think you're absolutely right. I'm not sure that we should try to understand, if we can get further than almost an affirmation, because we've worked together, we've seen each other so much, we respect what each other does. That's as far as I can get.

Jean   And that's enough.

Jack   Yes, it has to be for me. I have no other. But I think you're absolutely right to focus on that spiritual power. What was it Paul Tillich comments on in 'The Courage to Be'—the state of being grasped by the power of being itself. He was talking about the spiritual and religious experience, and that for me has summed it up.

As I understand it, 'action research' is a term used to refer to a way of working. Action research does not in itself offer a particular methodology. It is a term that communicates a special attitude by practitioners who hold certain values which they hope to realise in and through their work. Action research is not a thing; it is a concept, a term which refers to a particular approach. It is a metaphor, of which there are an increasing number of examples.

The characteristics of an action research approach may be easily recognised within the metaphor. I think the way in which people are currently working—the realisation of the metaphor—may be taken as 'action research' as it is practised.

Action research may be characterised as a way of working that

— is practitioner generated;
— is workplace oriented;
— seeks to improve something;
— starts from a particular situation;
— adopts a flexible trial and error approach;
— accepts that there are no final answers;
— aims to validate any claims it makes by rigorous justification processes.

IT IS PRACTITIONER GENERATED

Practitioners decide what they are interested in, what they want to study, how they want to approach it, how they intend to justify any statements they make about improving things, and what they want to do with their findings. Clearly this way of working cannot be isolationist. We all live and work in a pluralist society, and we have to adjust our lives to accommodate those of others. Although an action research approach starts with an individual looking critically at her or his own practice with a view to improving it, that exercise has to be placed realistically within the practical world of external (and internal) constraints, pressures and changing scenarios. Current questions within the movement include 'How can we move from 'I' to 'we'?'—that is, how can we develop our thinking to move away from a scenario of individual-oriented evaluation and modification of practice to one in which individuals agree a values base that can act as the foundation for a collective approach to sharing understanding how to improve practice (see Part Two, and the form of this text).

IT IS WORKPLACE ORIENTED

Action researchers ask questions about the here and now. They are trying to understand what is happening so that they can improve any unsatisfactory elements or celebrate good ones. This approach is quite different from a traditional 'scientistic' approach that aims to prove a hypothesis about someone else's situation. In an action research approach, I, the critically reflective practitioner, concentrate initially on my own situation, with the practical intent of changing it for the better, for the sake of myself and of others. I do not initially aim to enquire into other people's situations, to suggest to them how they might do things differently. I look first at myself, at putting my own house in order, and then I feel I am justified in communicating to others how I carried out my own process of self-improvement so that they may adopt and adapt my idea if they wish. They do not have to; there is no compulsion here. I aim to air and share ideas with others, not impose ideas on others. I publicly acknowledge that this is my way of working, which I am duty-bound to test out against the ideas of others in order to justify any claims I might make about improving my situation. I do not require others to take my ideas on board, unless they want to, in which case we then immediately form a community of like-minded, strategically-oriented practitioners.

By 'workplace oriented', I do not mean that an action research approach is applicable only to modes of technical production. It is applicable to situations in which people lead active, creative lives: in the home, in leisure pursuits, in bread-winning situations. This idea is resonant with MacIntyre's use of the term 'practice' to describe actions that are carried out as part of a practical community ethic (MacIntyre, 1981). I repeat that action research is not a 'thing' so much as a way of *doing* things, a way of living that incorporates certain values such as respect for others and their right to freedom, a desire for personal fulfilment of potential, and a love of peace and shared understanding. Workplace-oriented action research practices are those that translate the metaphor into the reality of the lives of people at work, rest and play; they try to make sense of what is happening here and now with a view to turning it into a situation in which the values they hold actually are realised. From saying that the world ought to be a more peaceful and productive place, they look at their own individual and collective situation to see how they actually can turn the world into a more peaceful and productive place. Action researchers look for ways in which they can get things done, here and now.

IT SEEKS TO IMPROVE SOMETHING

Action researchers are not content to accept an unsatisfactory situation, but make a personal commitment to improve it. The 'thing' that they decide to improve can vary from their own practice, their understanding of that practice, or the situation in which their practice is located. As mentioned above, the situation in which we work is often heavily influenced by social, economic, historical and other factors over which we have little or no control; and it is important, when considering adopting an action research approach for personal and professional development, that we recognise these factors for what they are and do not get frustrated by attempting to do too much. Advice given to budding action researchers (see for example, Kemmis and McTaggart, 1982) includes: 'Select an issue that you can realistically expect to do something about'. You can't change government policy—not immediately; but you can work systematically to persuading your immediate up-liner to look at things in a different way.

'Improve' is a value-laden term, and may often be implied to have negative elements: that things are bad to begin with. This is not an action researcher's mentality. An action researcher takes the view that life is a continual process of new beginnings and new questions. Life is creative, developmental, always on the move. The research report I produce is the story of my life so far, and indicates, as a prime value of that life, the desire to go on finding new and even better ways of living it. 'Better' is the operative word. It is a natural progression, in the evolutionary process of a dynamically creative lifestyle, that things will get better, whether they are already good or not; but nothing will ever be 'best', for that would then be an end to development. There are no final answers in an action researcher's repertoire—only provisional ones that are modified into new, more interesting questions (see below, Chapter 6).

IT STARTS FROM A PARTICULAR SITUATION

The insights developed by a person within one situation may be generalised to other people's situations. This is a different way of doing things than a traditional approach to research that says I have to draw conclusions (theories) about the world through observing how other people do things, and apply those conclusions to myself. The traditional way enables me to draw out a theory from the experience of others which I can use to guide the way I live. This is a 'theory guiding practice' approach.

As an example of this traditional view, if I am a mother, I can watch how other mothers treat their children, and apply their way to myself. I draw out a theory about mother-child relationships by observing the behaviour of other mothers. I demonstrate my faith in the theory by applying it to my own situation. A consequence is that, the more people demonstrate their faith in this way, the more the theory is legitimated, moving often towards a time when it will be accepted as a truth, unmodifiable and unchallengeable.

Action researchers begin from an alternative position in which they focus on a particular situation here and now, and try to understand it with a view to bringing about improvement. This way of making sense constitutes a process of *theorising* which is drawn out of practice (a 'theory generated through practice' approach).

The way in which I can develop a general theory about potential ways of doing things is by demonstrating publicly how I do things, explaining why I do as I do, and sharing my insights with others. I do not present this as a fixed theory. I present this as a possible way forward, and my attitude is such that all the while I hold the concept loosely. This is a provisional answer, a temporary answer, appropriate for as long as is necessary, but open to dismantling as soon as it is no longer appropriate, as the circumstances of my situation dictate. If a group of people wish to take my provisional theory and test it out for themselves within their own situation, then we may legitimately claim that we hold a certain theory; we share an insight into ways of getting things done. What is significant about an action research approach is that practitioners declare as a fundamental value the fluidity of the approach, the provisionality of any temporary theory they adopt for as long as it seems appropriate to their individual or collective context. An action research approach does not only imply drawing a theory out of practice. It also implies a critical reflection on a provisional theory; and a modification of the theory, and the process of theorising itself, as the situation requires.

IT ADOPTS A TRIAL AND ERROR APPROACH

Action researchers recognise fully that what may be appropriate for one person's situation is not necessarily so for another; and that what may be appropriate for a person at a particular time may not be so at another time. Life is a constantly changing network of constantly changing relationships. We have to accept this fact if we are to live the kind of life that we are striving for, in which we can all realise our values.

There is no one consistently 'right' way of doing things. Each situation, each set of relationships, has its own internal characteristics, all of which have to be understood in a way which is appropriate to the individual context. If one way does not seem to work, we try another. People who are able to adopt this approach (and an action research approach suggests that they do) are thinking and acting dialectically—that is, they are looking for the relationships and convergences that will help them to understand, accommodate, and accommodate to, the situation in which they find themselves. They are prepared to change themselves as well as seek to change the situation.

The trial and error methodology of action research is apparent in the published action research plans of workers in the field (see Chapter 3). The plans begin with a review of a particular situation, or set of situations, in which problems are identified; and they work systematically through phases of imagined solutions, action, evaluation, re-appraisal. . . The practitioner engages in episodes of action and reflection which, taken as a whole, may be characterised as self-reflective practice—reflection on action in action. Significant to this approach is that practice becomes a form of research, and research becomes a form of practice. Research is not an additional part; it is the form that our practice takes. An action research approach to life enables us to regard the whole way we live our life as a creative enterprise in which we are in control of our own destiny, so far as we are able in terms of the power relations that constrain us.

IT ACCEPTS THAT THERE ARE NO FINAL ANSWERS.

We can regard research as the telling of a particular story, in which things are changed as a result of certain experiences. Traditional ways of doing research offer us a completed story. We can read how someone did something and brought about certain results. It really is not possible to do that with action research. What is special about action research is that it allows people the flexibility to make up their own story as they go along. If one story line is not attractive, for whatever reason, it may be changed. There is no hard and fast plot; there are no characters to direct. The story evolves of its own accord. Traditional research is grounded in the story. Action research is grounded in the story-teller. There is no end, because each of us is too intent on making up the next bit to worry about what the end looks like. Each one of us is free to choose the song that we sing and how we sing it.

Freedom, however, can sometimes be hard to handle. I tend to the view that most of us like a structured environment. We are comfortable in knowing what we have to do and when we have to do it. We struggle against upheaval, and we make every effort to return to the familiar norm—signs of familiarity that offer the safety of trusted frameworks.

Even when the familiar is uncomfortable, we still tend to stay with it, for it is the known that we cherish, and the unknown, problematic way of life that we fear. Yet when the familiar becomes too uncomfortable, and generates a sense of tension in our minds, then we often feel we have to resolve the tension in order to re-establish harmony and equilibrium in our lives.

Adopting an action research approach can mean that life becomes problematic. It means that we have accepted that we want to change something that we are doing or that is being done to us, and we have made a commitment—in itself a hazardous undertaking. It means that from now on we have resolved to see things in a different way. What can be particularly threatening is that we are not sure what answers we are looking for—or, indeed, if there are any answers to be found. Often, when people first start their personal enquiries, they find that they are constantly discovering new questions instead of answers; and this can often be disturbing.

What is also discomfiting is the sense of responsibility that an action research approach imparts. I, the individual practitioner, am in control, inasmuch as my political, economic and cultural environment allows. I have to decide what is important in my practice, what is good and what needs attention. I have to decide how I am going to pay attention, to evaluate, to demonstrate publicly how I have improved things. I have to make a commitment to my own potential, to draw out my ability to make responsible judgements for myself, and to justify those decisions. It is no wonder that the world of action research is full of debate and debaters, given the sense of awe and wonder that its mode of personal freedom generates, along with the weight of being a responsible thinker who makes decisions about her own lifestyle which are bound to affect the lives of others.

Asking questions is hard; even harder is finding the right questions to ask. Following Collingwood (1939), I believe that there are no 'true' questions and answers; there are only 'right' questions and answers that will enable the dialogue to continue—that is, enable us to create new questions and answers. Traditional forms of research stress the need to find answers and aim for early closure. An action research approach stresses the need to find the right kind of questions that will help us to identify the best option.

IT AIMS TO VALIDATE ANY CLAIMS IT MAKES BY RIGOROUS JUSTIFICATION PROCEDURES.

Action research is an eminently common-sense approach to personal and professional development; so much so that, when people encounter the idea for the first time, they often say, "That's what I do in any case! What's different?"

What is different between adopting a general problem-solving approach to life and adopting an action research approach to life is that action research is a form of practice that carries a high profile in the public domain. You cannot do action research in isolation. You can do it unobtrusively, but you have to make your findings public, and you have to justify any claims you make that you have effected improvement as part of your personal enquiry. You have to be prepared to back up whatever you say with the proof of evidence.

Stenhouse (1983) says of research that it is a 'systematic enquiry made public'. An action research approach emphasises the systematic nature of the enquiry by helping us to develop an awareness of how each step is contingent upon another, and how each step develops and transforms itself. In order to protect our enquiries from accusations of woolliness or sloppy thinking, we have to communicate the rigorously systematic nature of our enquiry to others. This 'making public' may be small scale (telling a companion) or large scale (publishing in a journal).

Validation is one of the aspects of an action research approach that appears to be a vulnerable point that is quickly attacked by critics. Personally I do not see this as the case. In traditional forms of research it is easy to justify a claim that you have improved something, because there are criteria, such as performance indicators, that indicate a level of excellence. If you show that you can perform to an expected level you are judged successful. In an action research approach there are no such externally imposed criteria. If I say that I have improved something, I have to demonstrate the justification of that claim by pointing to the evidence of my own and other people's lives. I have to ask you to share with me specific criteria that we will agree are appropriate as 'indicators' of improved understanding and behaviour. We then have to interrogate the data of my practice—video and audiotape recordings, records, journals, field-notes—to see if the criteria are evident, and to see whether instances of the criteria—actual performances—support our claim that the participants in the enquiry have made progress. Our validation lies in our intersubjective agreement of the nature of improvement, and whether that improvement has in fact taken place. This process is anything but easy. It is indeed demanding, and calls for much debate between the validators themselves about the nature of the values they hold that enable them to share in the idea of the validation of individual and collective practices.

Jack   I still can't agree with you about what you understand by the educative relationship. It's the difficulty I have still of bringing certain experiences under my concept of education. It's strange this, because normally I would be relating almost everything to education. I would be trying to unify through my view of education. But on these issues which are much more to do with the spiritual and aesthetic sense, and also ethics, that's where the boundary becomes more blurred. When we get particularly to the spiritual dimension, the questions you asked me earlier are fundamental. You asked about the purpose and sense that we make of our own existence. I have made the point that I confront the certainty of my death and of yours, and the struggles I have had in confronting that certainty, and then coming through in a way that celebrates life and is life affirming. I'm still not able to subsume those experiences under my notion of education. I recognise that they inform, provide a motive power for whatever I do. That's all.

Jean   We are recognising that we all share common experiences and we enjoy these experiences. What we seem not to be agreeing on is actually what we call them.

Jack   I no longer want almost to engage. I want very much to accept whatever spiritual commitment you have, and I don't want to call it anything.

Jean   The naming is unimportant.

Jack   You can let me know in terms of Christian commitment, or whatever your motive power is; but there comes a point where I'd much sooner focus on ourselves and our relationships—our talk and our practical endeavours in the world, and recognise that those moments do exist that are intensely personal of how one confronts those certainties.

Jean   I share this sense of frustration when people try to define the concept of God and get quite upset at not being able to agree. One concept differs from another, and one gets caught up in this almost political thing that a particular definition is right, because that detracts from the overall enterprise of understanding of self, understanding how it is that we do as we do. But that doesn't help Moira in her research, in trying to understand and articulate the nature of the educative relationship.

Moira   No, it doesn't, but it does give me the insight that seems to have been growing recently that maybe it's a bit like action research—you can't actually characterise it. Maybe you can only be involved in it; maybe you can only experience it, or maybe you'll come to understand it in the sense of being involved in it as something that is educative. The work that I've been doing seems to have come to a complete stop. Last night I tried to write about it. I couldn't. That's rare. This morning I got up early and tried to write about it, and couldn't, and that's even rarer. Then it just struck me that perhaps (1) while I'm involved in an educative relationship I may not be able to characterise what that relationship is: maybe I can only ever do that retrospectively; (2) by even defining it, it will evaporate, and what I need to do is experience it and accrue the insights and the understandings from that which will enable me then to create better educative relationships in the future. Maybe the focusing and the emphasising is the educative relationship itself, is some kind of foil for me and is in fact not going to be the way forward. Maybe what I need to do is concentrate on the process of education, as opposed to the educative relationship.

Jack   That's similar to the conversation I was having with Erica yesterday. It is quite a struggle to tease out that idea of process; going through the experience. I think it's the focus on 'How do I do it better? How do I improve?' The idea of research comes in that we want to make the process public—reflecting on the experiences that you're having through time. That might be a better way.

Chapter Two

How will Action Research help me to know more?

Jack   I think there's a real power struggle going on as to what constitutes legitimate educational knowledge, and the form that educational enquiries take. On the one hand we had people like Peters and Hirst in the 1960s and 1970s wanting to impose their view of educational theory on teachers. On the other hand, we have practitioners like us who are keen to present our own accounts to demonstrate how we have come to understand our own practice in trying to live out our values in our work. Within the action research community itself I feel there is an ambivalence: there are those who subscribe to the logical form whereby they offer theories about the nature of research, and there are those like us who subscribe to the logical form whereby we regard practical work as the ground for drawing out personal theories of education. It is the form of the theory that is in question.

Ask yourself the following questions:

In terms of my personal and professional practice -

What do I know?
What do I need to know?
How will I find out?
How will I know that what I find out will be true?
How will I know that what I then know is enough?

It is possible to go on playing this game of 'I know that I know ...'; and the iterative quality inherent in the game highlights the problem that we are faced with when we are discussing issues to do with personal and professional knowledge. The idea of professional development is embedded in the idea of knowledge: What do I know, that I need to know more? How do I find out what I need to know? Where do I find the answers to my questions?

In order fully to understand the rationale for action research—how it has developed, and why, and how it enhances professional development—it is useful to look at some interesting basic aspects of epistemology—the knowledge base of personal and professional development.

1 The idea of knowledge

What follows here is a summary and extension of some ideas put forward in 'Teaching as Learning: an Action Research Approach' (McNiff, 1992).

Three questions serve as a starting point in discussing the idea of knowledge:

(a) What is the nature of knowledge?
(b) How is knowledge acquired?
(c) How is knowledge communicated?

(a) What is the nature of knowledge?

Probably the most popular conception of knowledge is that it is a body of facts or information that exists in sources of reference—books, databases, retrieval systems, maps, formulae, other people's minds. This kind of knowledge is usually termed 'objective knowledge' (Popper, 1972), and is usually characterised as 'know-that': I know that today is Friday. I know that this is a newspaper. There is another related form of knowledge referred to as 'know-how' (procedural knowledge): I know how to use a PCW. I know how to drive a car. There is some debate in the literature about whether there are these two kinds of knowledge or just one (for example, Ryle, 1949). What is important here is that we establish the fact that people often assume that knowledge exists in public form 'out there', independent of themselves.

This public, objectified knowledge, it is argued, may be judged to be true (verified) by referring to perceivable bits of evidence. I know that today is Friday because it says so on my calendar. I know that this is a newspaper because I can see it here in my hand. (There are other verification procedures based in categories such as linguistic analysis: I know that this is a newspaper because that is the symbol I give to the referent—but that discussion is not appropriate here.)

The assumption is that objective knowledge is grounded in what I perceive through my senses. Recourse to the data is the way to test out the truth of a claim to knowledge. When I say, "I know such and such", and someone says, "Prove it," I can point to the evidence as proof.

There is, however, another kind of knowledge altogether, which is referred to in the literature as 'personal knowledge' (Polanyi, 1958). Someone can ask me, "How do you know that today is Friday?" and I may respond, "Because it says so on my calendar"; but what do I say when someone asks me, "How do you know that you know?" I have no answer other than something like, "I don't know. I don't know how I know that I know. I just do." And then we get into the onion-peeling game, where each layer of 'I know' may be peeled back to reveal another layer of 'I know', and so on. At the end of the day we are left with a sure foundation of irrefutable yet non-demonstrable knowledge that is expressed simply in the words "I know". Those who believe that objective knowledge is the only form of legitimate knowledge assume that all knowledge may be categorised and accounted for: suppose that, if it were possible to give a number value to each piece of knowledge, it would be possible to add everything up and come out with a grand total. However, such a lump sum is non-achievable, because there is always the 'outer layer' question of 'How do you know that you know?' and this adds to the sum. So we are always adding to the grand total of public knowledge by adding our bit of personal knowledge to it. By definition, the sum of available knowledge can never be complete (see also Polanyi, 1969).

(b) How is knowledge acquired?

There are a number of different ways of coming to know. These include discovery and enquiry. One way to find things out is to ask someone else; another is to find out myself. Asking someone else results in my receiving certain information, via printed matter, the spoken word, or via many other media. Finding out myself means I have to fall back on my own understanding of my own experience. While it is true that there could be sub-divisions or extensions of these two ways which might suppose that, for example, I find out myself via the printed word, let us accept for a moment that I find out either via sources external to myself or internal to myself.

If we apply this notion to any field of human enquiry, we come up with a duality of who knows what. We have either (1) a knower who knows something, an object of knowledge, and passes her knowledge of that thing (information) on to someone who aspires to be a knower; or (2) we have a knower who independently aspires to know, and uses her aspiration to create knowledge (find out via her own experience).

If we apply this duality to any communicative situation between two or more persons, we come up with a situation in which (1) A passes on her knowledge of something to B, or (2) B creates her own knowledge and shares it with A. The difference here lies in a view of the nature of knowledge, and in patterns of communication. In (1), knowledge may be seen as information—public, external knowledge, knowledge *about* something rather than knowledge *of.* In (2) knowledge may be seen as our understanding of and commitment to the personal knowledge of our own experience. Consider, for example, that most of us know about the Queen, but few of us know her. Most of us have some knowledge about God, but we need to commit ourselves through an act of faith to know God. In terms of communication, in (1) communication may be seen as information processing—for example, let me tell you this so that you will know that ..., or know how .... In (2) it may be seen as the process of airing and sharing: let me tell you about the fact that I know God. I can tell you about my own knowledge, but only you can decide if you want to try for a similar form of knowledge by doing it yourself. I cannot know God for you, in the same way that you know yourself better than I know you. Only you have your own personal knowledge, and only I have mine; but we can talk together, share our understanding of our own knowledge, and we can pool our understanding and aim perhaps to externalise it—pass it on to others in a public form—so that it goes into the public domain as a legitimate form of communal knowledge.

(c)   How is knowledge communicated?

The process of communication is grounded in the idea of practical intent. If I don't intend to do something with the knowledge, to use it in some way, I don't bother to communicate it. The way in which people communicate with intent—use their knowledge—reflects the views already discussed about the nature of knowledge and its acquisition.

In recent years there has been a significant shift in a view of the nature of professional knowledge, and in ways of coming to know, or forms of enquiry.

Traditional forms of enquiry have been based largely on an information-processing model; that is, input-output:

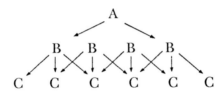

input of information →KNOWER→ output of information

The underlying assumption is that the kind of knowledge that is regarded as legitimate is of the publicly available kind—that is, objective knowledge.

Traditional patterns of professional development operate via similar attitudes, in a line-management mode: within the hierarchy, someone with power tells someone with lesser power what to do and how to do it.

It is not difficult to see that, within such a scheme, professional expertise is a case of coming up to an externally imposed standard, often consisting of specific performance indicators, which constitute a pass-fail divide. In this way, it is assumed that, if I want to find out something to do with my own performance, I have to consult an external authority. Even if I want to find out what it is I ought to *know,* I have to ask a supervisor, consult a book to find out *about* things via someone else's knowledge. In this way, the traditional view has been that a specific theory has offered guidance about how I ought to do things: I have taken someone else's theory, and I have fitted my practice to it.

How, then, do I communicate personal, subjective knowledge? We have already established that it is impossible for one person to have access to another person's inner knowledge save through commitment. I cannot know your thoughts as you do; I cannot feel your toothache, or your joy, or your fear, except through empathising with you, establishing with you a relationship such that we each attempt to enter and dwell in the other's mind, in order to create intersubjective agreements about our experience.

I can communicate my personal knowledge to you only if you commit yourself to believing in me and my knowledge.

So communicating personal knowledge lies not in a process of telling but of *imagining*. Its action is not the passing on of information so much as arranging the conditions in which agreements may be reached. Those conditions are vital, and are grounded in certain shared values, as noted above:—respect for the other, love of individual freedom, rejection of power relationships. The reason for agreeing to establish those conditions is the practical intent of acting in the other's best interest, to bring about a more peaceful and productive world.

In conclusion to this part, I can say that the debate about the nature, acquisition and communication of knowledge rests on the idea of 'the knower and the known' (Grene, 1969). In one view, I am an active knower, the creator of my own knowledge. The 'known' is my own understanding of that which I perceive via my senses. I make sense of the world, and offer my interpretation to others for their scrutiny.

In a traditional view, I am the recipient of other people's knowledge. They understand the world and communicate that understanding to me. By extension, I am the object of their knowledge, because I am part of the world that they profess to know. The 'known' is what they choose to pass on to me. I make sense of the world via other people's interpretations.

It is not hard to see that the idea of power relations is implicit in this second view. Probably because of the emergence of increasingly democratic forms of social organisation over the last century, there has been a substantial critique of the forms of enquiry that are considered legitimate. Over the last few decades in particular there has been a revolution in ways of thinking about the idea of practitioners' knowledge, and today there is an active challenge from people at the grassroots levels of professional endeavour against the 'ivory tower' attitude of those who consider themselves 'professional knowers'. In the next section I want to look at the form of this critique, what it looks like when it is acted out in the lives of real people, and suggest new directions it looks to be taking.

2. The idea of professional development.

Let me now relate the idea of knowledge to the idea of professional development, and draw a parallel between forms of enquiry and forms of professional development. I shall suggest that traditional forms of enquiry offer a framework for traditional forms of skills training, and that emergent dialectical forms offer a grounding for democratically-oriented forms of personal enquiry.

I shall explore the same duality as in the previous section, starting with slightly different questions:

(a) What constitutes professional development?
(b) How is professional development acquired?
(c) How is professional development communicated?

Before tackling the questions, however, let me bring in a new perspective, and say that the two views discussed so far may be contrasted in terms of their methodology, their logic and their intent.

Methodology

As noted above, the methodology usually applied in traditional schemes of professional development is a linear management model where a powerful knower arranges for specific inputs which are intended to produce desired outcomes (If I do this, then that will happen). Within the programme, the manager guides the practice of trainees, offering a theory and a set of conditions that are assumed to guarantee success if they are executed in a consistent fashion.

It is not difficult to see this view at work within dominant market-oriented forms of training. The emphasis is on performance indicators, standardised tests, vocational qualifications—all instruments which are grounded in a view of technical excellence. In today's technocratic society, skills are tops, and training programmes focusing on the 'correct' performance of professionals are to be valued and supported (note the pending 1992 legislation on adult education: my Monday evening GCSE psychology class should continue to be subsidised; my Tuesday evening 'Introduction to philosophy and psychology' will not. Examination courses lead to vocational qualifications; 'leisure' [education-oriented?] courses lead to an enrichment of life that cannot be [and need not be] encapsulated in a certificate.)

The paradox within this approach is that professionals are systematically de-professionalised. Far from building up the wisdom critically to evaluate practice, they are encouraged to aspire to a level of technical expertise which is not necessarily related to their own sense of what constitutes good professional practice. They are encouraged by their managers to become efficient at applying public knowledge—to become expert technicians— rather than develop a sense of confidence in the personal knowledge they need to develop in order to improve their level of wise awareness.

A reactionary view, and this includes an action research approach, which currently offers the most systematic form within alternative methods of enquiry, encourages practitioners to see themselves as creators of their own practice. It does this by offering a methodology of question and answer (a dialectical form) that is designed to elicit the practitioner's best understanding how to deal with the issue of professional self-development (see Chapters 3 and 4). In adopting this form of enquiry, the practical wisdom in action of professionals is highlighted as the ground for their own process of development. Instead only of drawing on the theories of others and applying those theories to their own work, practitioners are entitled critically to consider their own practice, and to draw conclusions about how best to solve problems by trying to account for why they are doing as they are.

Logic

Logic refers to the way in which people organise their thoughts, or think about thinking.

The logical form of theory that is grounded in a view of the legitimacy of public, objectified knowledge (an *empiric* approach) is called propositional. Propositional logic takes the form 'If X ..., then Y .... ': "If I do this, then that will happen". If I conduct an enquiry in this way, I begin with the assumption that I hold certain hypotheses about the world which I can then set out to prove. An example of this approach would be "I believe that people will learn more efficiently if I put them through certain training exercises". I then set up training exercises, and I keep records of my subjects' performance over time to see if my programme works. I conduct experiments on people to see if they will perform in the way which I think they will. I make predictions about the world, and I run tests to see if they will come true. Indeed, I might so arrange conditions in such a way as to make sure that they do come true.

The logical form of practitioner-centred enquiry lies in the process of question and answer—that is, a dialectical form that traces relationships along the manifold strands of the web. It finds its meaning in the questions that practitioners ask about how they can improve the quality of their own work, and often takes the form 'How can I improve ... ?' The living 'I' (Whitehead, 1989b), that is, the person conducting the enquiry, is the focus of the enquiry. I can say that the subject, 'I', am researching my own practice, 'I'. Mine is an enquiry by the self of the self. It is geared to self-knowledge, and seeks to establish a knowledge base to improve practice through the process of asking questions.

Intent

The intent of a researcher who is engaged in an empiric enquiry (that takes public objectified knowledge as a foundation, that aims to find out about others) is to prove an hypothesis. History shows us that people who adopt this approach then often use this 'proven' factual knowledge base to control the activities of others by requiring them to conform to that knowledge base. For example, I in my role as manager of a shop may believe that my customers will buy more if all my employees are dressed in uniform, imparting a sense of solidarity and identity. I therefore require all my employees to conform. I know best, and I require them to accept that I do. At home, in my role as a parent, I believe that I know what is best for my children, and I require them to accept my authority, and to do as they are told. The inherent assumption in adopting this way of life is that there is a non-negotiable truth, a 'right way'. This is a view of people who tend to a view that knowledge exists independent of human minds.

The intent of a researcher who is engaged in a personal enquiry is to ask questions about her practice with a view to developing her personal knowledge of that practice. She then uses this knowledge to demonstrate the improvement of practice as a justification for the way that she undertakes her work/life, with the practical intent of sharing that knowledge with others so that they, too, may ask questions that will help them to develop their work/life. The form of communication of this kind of knowledge is dialogue. The formation of dialogical communities (Bernstein, 1983, 1991)—that is, communities that take dialogue as their form of communication—facilitates the sharing and developing of personal knowledge as a community ethic.

Let me return now to the questions I posed at the beginning of this section.

(a) What is the nature of professional development?

Empiricists (those who believe in the power of public, externally-oriented knowledge) tend to the view that professional development is an observable process in which practitioners show an increasing amount of expertise. This expertise may be characterised in terms of performance indicators, competencies, and skills. Their performance rating may be seen in terms of checklists, 'can do' indices, and norm-referenced testing procedures. These testing procedures take the form of standardised assessment tasks, in which the end product of expertise is clearly formulated. Increasing professionalism, in this view, is geared towards early closure: that is, the pathway to ultimate success is clearly laid out, and full development is judged to have been reached at a certain level/stage. Tests in this mode operate on a pass-fail basis.

Rationalists (those who believe in the power of personal, individual-oriented knowledge) believe that professional development is a transformational process in which the practitioner develops in practical wisdom. Wisdom is not something which may be defined in terms of significant features, nor which may be observed to develop as part of a structured process. Wisdom is a paradox (Sternberg, 1990), a knowledge that one does not know, that one is always in process of coming to know. Wisdom is the quality of thought that allows one critically to evaluate the process of thinking itself. The more I acknowledge that I still have much to know, the more I grow in professional wisdom. The more I am prepared to learn, to be open to my own sense of process, the more competent I am as a professional.

COMMENT

When I visit my dentist I hope and pray that he knows what he is doing. Each visit is an act of faith, that he has attended the latest training courses, read the most recent technical journals, has bought in the latest technology. After all, it is *my* teeth. When I visit my dentist I am a full-blooded empiricist.

Yet, on reflection, am I committed only to my faith in his technical expertise? Do I not also value with all my heart that he understands my fear, that he has a funny picture on the ceiling above the chair, that he is considerate in getting the crown made on time? These are qualities of a personal nature, to do with establishing a rapport with me that we trust each other as fellow-professionals and fellow-human beings. What price his technical excellence if I am too scared to go to him?

In my opinion, our Western culture is dominated by a view of professional development as technical excellence. Too little importance is given to the personal development in which professional development is grounded. I hope, throughout my project, to persuade colleagues of my own conviction that professional development is a process in and through which we improve the quality of life for ourselves and others, and not just a process in which we learn to jump through other people's hoops. We need to get the balance right. At the moment, I feel, there is far too much emphasis on requiring professionals to be expert technicians. The need for personal development is put into the shadow. We need to strive towards a situation where professionals are primarily caring people, and *consequently* care enough to develop their technical expertise to a level at which they can then improve the quality of life for others, in and through their technique. Technical excellence is a tool we use, as caring professionals, in the service of others. It is not an end in itself.

(b) How is professional development acquired?

If we operate from a view of professionalism as technical expertise, the way in which it is acquired is for the practitioner to gain access to sources that will offer her the information she is seeking. This culture of supply and demand views professional development as a 'collection' process. As I go on in my professional life I 'collect' bits of development, as I would collect credits to add to my professional portfolio. I add to my basket of eggs—one from a course on management, one on technical aspects of my subject, one on interpersonal skills, and so on.

Now, there is nothing wrong with this approach, provided it is seen for what it is and kept in perspective. Accreditation/assessment of prior learning schemes operate like this, where a practitioner offers previously unrecognised modules of professional learning as credit towards a wider course of study. The problem arises, in my view, when this attitude towards professional development dominates to the exclusion of other views, including a view of professional development that is grounded in the raising of awareness of individuals of their own potential for previously untried ways of doing things.

Here I am arguing for the need for critical thinking to be placed in high profile within schemes of professional development. Critical thinking is a way of looking at things that is based on reconstruction. By this I mean the following:

When I acquire a piece of knowledge, either from the public world of papers, television, and other media, or from the private world of my own understanding, I immediately question its truth. This does not mean that I dismiss the piece of knowledge as unreliable. It means that I test it, I evaluate it, against criteria of validity, honesty, true representation, appropriateness, and so on (see Habermas, 1979). I critically evaluate it by taking it to pieces, so to speak, *deconstructing* it, to see if the piece of knowledge holds together as a synthetic whole. Take, for example, that I see a report on television about allegations of sexual harassment brought by a woman against a prominent male. I need to ask myself questions such as, 'Are the accusations justified or do they appear imbalanced? Is the language used to report the case unbiased, or full of innuendo? Are the circumstances surrounding the public presentation handled with sensitivity by the media, or does hysteria creep in anywhere?' I need to ask a hundred questions like this. Recent reports suggest that Sir Cyril Burt was possibly not so much a victim of his own prefabrication as of the media scandalmongers of the time who were after a sensational story. It could be not so much the case that he presented the facts falsely as that *they* did. Deconstruction means teasing out the strands of the compacted ball of material, systematically isolating each thread and examining its form. If I, in humility and compassion, express the fact that I am satisfied that the material meets the standards of integrity that my criteria require (mine and those of companions with whom I am in dialogue), I then proceed to *reconstruct*—that is, put it back together again within the new framework of my own understanding. The process of critical thinking constitutes on-going deconstruction and reconstruction, and it is a form of thinking being used increasingly in an action research approach (see Chapter 3).

This, in my view, is the starting point for schemes of professional development. Before even embarking on aspects to do with the acquisition of technical know-how, we need to accept the high priority of the need for practitioners to think critically. And even before we ask practitioners critically to evaluate their professional development, we need to help them to get to grips with the basic idea of *thinking*. Professional development is grounded in personal development; and personal development is not an 'add on' procedure so much as a lifelong transformation of understanding.

To accept this view, however, of the 'acquisition', perhaps better rephrased as the transformation of professional development, is to accept the inevitable implication that traditional schemes of input-output line management processes are inadequate. So, what are the alternatives?

(c) The communication of professional development

Currently dominant forms of communication operate in the traditional format of 'If ... , then ... ': if I tell you this, then you can apply it. I pass on the information; you receive it, apply it to yourself, and I sign your form to say that you have completed that module. The relationship between us is one of power: I know; I tell you that, and what, you ought to know.

My own view about communicative relationships is that they are guided by the attitudes towards power of the participants within those relationships. If I set myself up as the knower, and you subscribe to this view, we both legitimate my knowledge and my right to be a knower (and you forfeit your right to make your personal claim to knowledge). If, alternatively, we both agree that we begin from an initial starting point that we each respect the other's personal knowledge, without the need to exert power over the other, we can both engage in an equal partnership of discourse.

If this view is applied to schemes of professional development, it is immediately apparent that roles and power relationships undergo a radical change from their traditional forms (see Chapter 5). We have to abandon a 'teacher and taught' relationship, as well as 'right and wrong' attitudes towards professional knowledge. We have to change the teaching mode from the delivery of a scheme of work to the discussion of personal insights into workplace situations. In-service training gives way to professionals' education; delivery gives way to sharing. Monologue transforms itself into dialogue.

Further, the spirit in which these relationships are fostered has to be one of generosity and respect. As a person with the responsibility for professionals' continuing education, I must not accept this transformation of role with a begrudging relinquishing of power, as if I have to bow to the changing times and get on with it. I have to see, fundamentally, that I need actively to put myself into a learning mode, in order best to communicate to my clients that they, too, are in a learning mode. The way in which I ensure the continuing professionalisation of my clients is, first, to attend to my own, in the surety that this is the way to establish the kind of educative relationship that will help them to blossom where they are planted.

Chapter Three

How do I learn how to do Action Research?

Jean   I think this is where this form of thought - our group - has a particularly strong contribution to make. I think the really powerful contribution lies not in the offering of this way of thinking as an orthodoxy. Some people could look at it like that - that we are requiring people to adopt this form of thinking. The power of this form is that it really is emancipatory, because of itself it lets people exercise their power of freedom to question the form, and in that I think it is unique. This is where the idea of the 'good order' of the form lies for me, in that it is not a coercive form.

Jack   That is the difference I feel between what we're doing and what I experience in my dealings with other people in other parts of the country. At that conference I was telling you about, I felt that I was going back into the coercive form. Now, I think that the generative form, because it has got that break in the sense that it cannot rest upon what I, for example, say, is particularly powerful. We might agree that I've originated one idea about educational theory being constituted by the descriptions and explanations that you and I produce for our own practice. That is, I think, an original thought, but it is a liberating one in the sense that I can't impose on others to create a form of practice that is not grounded in their own intentionality.

Jean   You see, this is the same problem that Gorbachev had. You enable other people to exercise their own freedom such that they can exercise that freedom against you. This is the old paradox of freedom, of liberating people, and you take on that responsibility when you enter the game.

This chapter is in two parts: first, what advice the literature offers in terms of how to do action research; second, advice on how to use the advice that the literature offers. I want to point out how the literature recommends that action research may be used as a form of critique, and then I want to encourage you to apply your own critique to those recommendations. I am endorsing my own view that action research is an approach that helps people to question. (My argument may be carried through to advise you to critique the fact that I am advising you in the first place. For that, however, we have to enter into personal dialogue, which is not immediately possible in the distance mode that printed documents impose. However, when we meet in person, or communicate directly, we may discuss just the issues I am raising here.)

1.   GUIDANCE IN THE LITERATURE

The guidance in the literature on how to do action research does vary, and the specific methodology you choose will depend on which approach you find most appropriate to your way of thinking and your own situation. The literature offers us basically two approaches—the one developed at the University of East Anglia, and the other developed at the University of Bath. Both these efforts have been developed within the field of education.

Both initiatives share the same rationale—to put the practitioner at the centre of the research enterprise—and the same intent—to redefine educational theory whereby the reality of teachers' practices embody educational theory. My own view is that the two types also incorporate hidden agendas which are reflections of their originators' view of the power relations between teachers and teacher educators; but this is to anticipate.

It would be useful here briefly to trace the origins of action research as we know it, and to see how it has gained as a credible approach to professional development. This will be a brief review, for I have already covered this ground in detail (McNiff, 1988). I will then go on to show the difference between the approaches, how they may be applied, and point to the sort of practical advice they offer.

A brief history of the evolution of action research.

Action research was a term created by, among others, Kurt Lewin (1946), a social psychologist working in America. He offered a basic action plan for the improvement of practice through observation, a reconnaissance of any problems, a proposed solution to the problems, an implementation of the proposed solution, an evaluation to see if the solution was effective, and a subsequent modification of practice. This constituted an action-reflection cycle, which could then be applied repeatedly by the practitioner to move the situation closer towards a desired outcome.

Action research was popularised in Britain within the teaching profession. It has been said that academics 'hi-jacked' the idea to describe and explain their own practice in supporting classroom teachers. This appropriation by academics appears in fact to have secured a place for action research as a legitimate form of enquiry, and I now want to elaborate on the suggestion that the work that has been done mainly within education as a profession is eminently transferable in and across other professions. I will also make the point in Chapter 4 that education should not be seen as the exclusive territory of the teaching profession, but as a concept that overspills everywhere. Indeed, I do believe that the professions need to take on the responsibility for the continuing education (not only training) of their practitioners, with all the uncomfortable implications of the re-negotiation of power relationships and the agreement for intersubjective understandings. More of this later.

Action research had been going for some time in Britain before it was given the name 'action research', in the sense that, during the massive curriculum-change process that was under way in the 1960s and 1970s with a move towards comprehensive education, teachers began to question the ethos of a mainly academic curriculum that was geared towards the success of brighter children in public examinations at the age of 15/16 (Elliott, 1991). This led to substantial school-based reform. The curriculum reform movement generated new conceptions of teaching and learning, and evaluation began to become an exercise of discussing and justifying personal practice with colleagues, rather than looking to the judgement of an external observer.

In the 1970s, the movement was given focus and direction by the establishment of the Humanities Curriculum Project under the direction of Lawrence Stenhouse of the University of East Anglia. This project stressed the need for the practical wisdom of teachers to be at the heart of pedagogic practices; and gave prominence to the concept of 'teacher as researcher' (Stenhouse, 1975), a concept which has since been a central tenet in the action research enterprise.

Stenhouse gathered round him a band of academics who have since gone their separate ways, but who all shared a common sense of purpose in promoting the idea of professional development being grounded in practical learning (Rudduck, 1991). Some of these people articulated and formalised the principles of action research (as it came to us from Lewin) as a system that could reflect, in a theoretical form, the practical actions of teachers as they tackled problematic issues.

At the same time, Jack Whitehead at the University of Bath was working with groups of teachers in Local Education Authorities, supporting them as they tried to find the right questions that would help them to make sense of their problematic practice, questions of the kind, 'How do I improve this process of education here?'

The benefit that this movement has brought to teachers is that, in principle, they are empowered to be in control of their own practice, and freed from the theory-driven model that imposes ideal standards towards which they must aim. Both schools of thought have translated this fundamental value into practicalities, in the sense that there are published schemes available to help teachers work through their practice with a view to improving it. The form of these action planners, however, is quite different, and I think this is a very important point. I think the way in which the planners are devised reflect the intentions of their authors, and that this is symptomatic of the wider issue of what counts as valid knowledge.

Let me take a brief look at the types of action plan available in the literature and the accompanying advice. One type of action plan offers clear guidance in the form of action steps: the sort of behaviour to adopt. The other type offers clear guidance in the form of questions to ask: the sort of attitude to adopt. All published forms of action planner follow the basic action-reflection sequence of 'observe—reflect—plan—act—evaluate—modify', this sequence to be repeated as the need of the individual practitioner impels.

Structured approaches

The best known plans of this kind are found in Kemmis and McTaggart (1982), 'The Action Research Planner', and Elliott (1981, 1991), which offer a step-by-step guide. They offer procedural guidelines for teachers and administrators interested in improvement and change in their schools. They provide a way of thinking systematically about what happens in schools or classrooms, implementing action where improvements are thought to be possible, and monitoring and evaluating the effects of the action with a view to continuing the improvement.

I have presented and critiqued the plans elsewhere (McNiff, 1988) on the grounds that this behavioural orientation is not intrinsically educational and does not necessarily lead to enhanced understanding. As a teacher-educator, I do not think I help my colleagues to develop their practical wisdom by telling them what to do, requiring that they model *my* pedagogical behaviour, or offering answers, drawn from my own experience, which I require them to apply to theirs (though I am happy to share the insights I have drawn from my own research). Rather, I encourage them to think with their own minds about their own situation, and to speak with their own voices about how they can improve it. I cushion them against the risk involved when their critical thinking makes them see things in a new, uncomfortable light, the sense of alienation when old assumptions are critiqued and rejected (Brookfield, 1987); but I do not cushion them against their experience of their own experience.

In order to work this way, I choose a strategy of asking opportunistic questions, supposing that the answers to the questions will be embodied in the transformations that practice undergoes. My procedure of questioning itself involves arranging for my clients to ask their own questions.

Dialectical approaches

(a) The work of Jack Whitehead

The second kind of action plan available incorporates this kind of questioning mentality. Jack Whitehead has developed a question-oriented approach that is now widely used in programmes of professional development.

He begins with his own action plan:

1. I identify a problem when some of my educational values are denied in my practice;

2. I imagine a solution to the problem;
3. I act in the direction of the solution;
4. I evaluate the solution;
5. I modify my ideas and my practice in the light of the evaluation.   (Whitehead, 1985, 1989a & b)

This action plan does not aim to offer substantive answers, but indicates a pathway along which certain gates may be opened to allow access to many new scenarios. The plan has been tried, tested and adapted by many practitioners (for example, Eames, 1990; Larter, 1989). It has also been incorporated into aspects of award-bearing courses of the University of Bath, in terms of a set of questions that can act as the basis for an individual's action enquiry:

1. What is your concern?
2. Why are you concerned?
3. What do you think you could do about it?
4. What kind of 'evidence' could you collect to help you make some judgement about what is happening?
5. How would you collect such 'evidence'?
6. How would you check that your judgement about what has happened is reasonably fair and accurate?

The plan, and variations of it, is being used extensively in programmes of teacher education (for example, Avon LEA, 1990). As noted above, most work here has been done in mainstream education, and Whitehead has focused his enquiry on the *educational* nature of educational enquiry. The implication here is that the form of the plan itself is highly generalisable to the all-embracing concept of professional development (see also Chapter 4). We need to start with the notion, as Whitehead does, of what constitutes the 'good order' of a particular community of professionals; how they see the constitution, acquisition and use of the 'good order' as embodying the evolution of their society; and, through their personal and professional knowledge, how they attempt to make explicit for themselves the values that they hold implicitly within the notion of the 'good order'.

Because this book is part of the project to disseminate the ideas that have been developed at the University of Bath, it is worthwhile giving here a brief outline of the main features of Jack Whitehead's thought (for a fuller exposition, see McNiff, 1992, Chapter 3).

Whitehead places the individual enquirer at the centre of human enquiry. We need to acknowledge the living 'I' as the epistemic centre, he maintains, otherwise educational researchers are in danger of producing propositional theories which do not directly relate to educational practice. We need to acknowledge the force of the individual consciousness in interpersonal relationships in order to understand the nature of our commitments, and to work towards establishing the good order of a rational society.

I must also acknowledge myself as a living contradiction, says Whitehead. When I say that I believe in something, and then I do the opposite, I exist as a living contradiction. When I say I should not steal, and then I do, I am not living up to my own beliefs. I think we would all recognise this experience.

As an educator, I hold a number of educational values. Within my practical, everyday workplace situation, the potential which is embodied in those values is often denied. Educational enquiry, for Whitehead, is a way in which this negation may be overcome, with the practical intent of enabling me to live out my educational values in my practice and realise my full potential.

It is worth noting here that the idea of realising and living out my educational values in my practice does not mean the imposition of my values on you. It means that each one of us recognises the quintessential integrity of our living 'I's', and, through airing and sharing our values, we make explicit a sense of vision that we may come to the position where we may develop a common sense of purpose and strategic action (Habermas, 1981) to improve the quality of education for ourselves and for the people in our care. In this sense, action research works towards the best interest of the other, and its methodology is dialogue (see Chapter 4).

(b) The work of Jean McNiff

My own work is interlinked with that of Jack Whitehead, and equally focuses on the need for educators to enable practitioners to develop as critical thinkers. I am particularly interested in trying to characterise the nature of the cognitive forms that enable us to build theories about how understanding is facilitated. I have called this enterprise:

The generative order of educational knowledge

Imagine that you are a magician of infinite power. Imagine that, at a word, you could put into effect a process whereby every thing in the world started changing of its own accord into a different kind of thing, that was recognisably the same original thing, but that became more mature with each step in the process of change. Seeds started turning into plants, raindrops formed oceans, students became professors, one-man bands metamorphosed into orchestras.

The power that you have unleashed is called generative power (see also Chapter 6). The processes that it begins are called transformational processes. Imagine that each thing in the world contains its own blueprint of what it could be—a sunflower seed turns into a sunflower, left to its own devices—but no thing will actually fulfil its own potential unless the generative power is available. The transformational processes at work in the world are grounded in the power of generativity. The number systems of the world are really meaningless unless I start using them to calculate, and I can perform an infinite number of calculations. The rules of language are meaningless unless I use them to create new language.

Now imagine that you want to teach other magicians how to use their power of generative creativity. Your own generative power has to work actively within you, otherwise you deny your own potential as a magician of infinite power. You show them the secret of setting the power in motion, and, by inevitable implication, they return the compliment, showing you the secret of their power. This is truly a magic circle whereby the power within you itself transforms your own community into a better, more fully-realised version of itself.

Now, transfer the analogy to the real you, in relationship with others. Consider how your individual life is transformed into a better version of itself, provided you are part of a community, each of whom acts in the other's best interest. This sort of community may be encouraged by each of you because you want to improve your own community, and spread the word into the wider world to show that it can be done and that you have done it by working together. You know how you have done it by working together, and you share the knowledge.

These are the elements within my own project. I take the idea of generative power as the basic unit of energy whereby each thing may transform itself endlessly in the process of its own realisation of potential. In terms of the educational enterprise, I see the development of educational knowledge as being the process of an individual's ever-expanding consciousness, which is encouraged by the parallel processes of other expanding consciousnesses with which I am in conversation. The development of our individual and collective understanding helps us to promote the evolution of our own society, each acting in the other's best interest. The generative power at work in me has the potential to transform the world, but only through the will of others who are equally aware of their own potential.

2. ACTION RESEARCH AS CRITIQUE

The idea of critique has been articulated intermittently throughout this text. I want to focus now on critique as a living element in a living theory—that is, to help you, the living reader, to develop your own power of rational thought so as to see other people's theories (and that includes this book, as it constitutes my present best thinking) for what they are: the product of thought that thinkers are offering as a resource to help colleagues develop their thought.

The idea of critique

Take the well-known example of Orwell's 'Animal Farm'. Mr Jones ran Manor Farm in a brutal manner and oppressed the animals severely. Finally, the animals overthrew Jones, and set up their own government, maintained by the pigs, who then set out to strengthen their image of the ruling intellectual class. Over time, the pigs transformed the embryonic democracy that had been the spur to the revolution into a dictatorship where they oppressed the other animals severely.

This is the same process that could possibly happen in an ideology critique (the activity of questioning an ideological system that is already well established). A set of ideas (SI), incorporating a view of the human condition, is judged to be the 'right' way. Certain radicals disagree, and discredit and reject the set of ideas (SI), and propose instead an alternative set of ideas (ASI). (ASI) becomes accepted as the norm, and, over time, its transitional character as a possible temporary alternative transforms into that of a fixed permanent way. The alternative that was offered with a sense of diffidence and caution is now reified (fixed), and abstracted from the consciousness of the radicals who created it, to exist as an impersonal system that assumes control over the society of which the radicals are a part.

Imagine now that a second group of activists propose yet another set of alternative ideas (ASAI), and instigate a revolution to discredit (ASI), and instal (ASAI) in its place. How do they check that (ASAI) will not go the same way to reificiation as (SI) and (ASI)? Where is the fail-safe mechanism that stops the process plunging into degeneration?

There are a number of ways of dealing with the problem, mainly:

1. The empiric-objectivist way, where a society agrees norms and standards which are then used to test the truth claims within a given set of assumptions. This is the way of, for example, the logical positivists who held that truth conditions rest in verification: I can say something is true if I demonstrate through factual evidence the verification of its internal truth.

2. The relativist way, where a society agrees that its constituent members are entitled to establish their own truth relative to their particular circumstances and contexts. This truth is then put to the test of a factual analysis of the contexts which the claim to truth allegedly reflects.

3. The dialogical-dialectical way, where a society agrees the right of each of its constituent members to make his or her own truth claim. Members justify their claim by demonstrating their 'version of truth' through the way that they live—that is, they attempt actively to live out their values. They offer their way of life, as an embodiment of their truth claim, to be validated by the community of which they are a part. This validation is through the process of dialogue.

The objectivist and the relativist ways are susceptible to reification. The dialogical way resists reification, because its substantive categories of concern (*what* people agree—the truth claims of its members) are in a process of constant transformation; and its forms of cognition (*how* people agree—the agreed process for reaching agreement)—is also inherently transformational. To expand: freedom of thought by definition must be free, in the content of the thought produced, in the forms of thinking employed, and in the right of the individual thinker to exercise his or her own freedom of thought. Dialogical communities must by definition be grounded in dialogue—that is, the process of reaching intersubjective agreement through rational argument with the practical intent of human betterment.

The idea of critique rests here. It does not rest in the imposition of one form on another, or in the rejection of one form in favour of another. Then the process of critique itself becomes a reified structure. The idea of critique rests in the openness of individuals who nurture the quality of openness throughout their society, and their agreement not to violate the integrity of the other through selfish moves towards closure.

These ideas enter into the consistent theme that, in order to enlarge upon our own ability to decide how best to develop our own professionalism, we need to develop our critical faculties, and to turn that faculty back on itself in order to understand our own practical intent in deciding to use this critical form. We need not only to construct our theories of professional development, but also then systematically to deconstruct them, with a view to reconstucting our actions as a reflection of the values that have underpinned the process of critical reflection, through critical dialogue.

In conclusion, let me say that action research is a way of using personal understanding to look at personal understanding. It is a way to question norms and taken-for-granteds, but, in order to use it in this critical way, we have to turn action research back on itself and use it to justify our very use of it. We have to hold up to the mirror our decision to use action research, and use one reflected decision to justify the other.

In effect, for a research programme to be called educational, in the sense that I, the practitioner, may develop my own story as I go along, I need to develop insights into the process of developing insights, to be aware of my own process of awareness. I need to use my action enquiry to explore the process of action enquiry.

This, in my opinion, is the ultimate power of action research. As noted above, to try to reduce the idea of action research and present it as a method is to deny its very epistemological base, the pushing back of the frontiers of knowledge. It is not that action research offers a critique; it is that the *idea* of action research offers a critique. For it is in following through my sense of vision that I am able to develop that I actually *do* develop. Grasping the idea of action research helps me to appreciate that all doors are potentially open, and that I have the key that will open them.

Chapter Four

How do I become an Action Researcher?

Jean   So, if I have a talent I use the talent that I'm given. To me, that's the essence of moral endeavour—actively to strive to realise the potential of which you are capable.

Jack   Suppose I've got the potential, Jean, to be a villain. Now I've got this great potential—and people have got enormous potential sometimes for evil—and I can realise this. The worry I have is that, on the views that you were just expressing there, you never come to the good order.

Moira   I'm not following what you're saying.

Jack   Jean's point is, we have almost a moral responsibility to develop our talent.

Moira   Yes.

Jack   To me, the problem is undoubtedly that many people seem to have talents for —

Moira   Oh! I see what you mean! This point always has to be re-emphasised for me because I always make the assumption that we're inherently good. People do say, 'Yes, but what about those who are actually not going to do things for the social good, that don't care about democracy, the integrity of the individual?' and so on, and I have to think, 'Oh, yes, there are some people for whom that is a reality.' I always have to be reminded of that.

Jean   I share this with you. I have been accused in the past of being naïve because I do have this assumption of the inherent goodness of people. And I must always caution myself, because what you say there, Jack, is the accusation that is sometimes levelled against people and against action research as a movement, that it is a fairly naïve approach—the assumption that things are going to go well; and I am aware that I must always put this in the provisional context of acting in other people's best interests. Provided we have that sort of underlying agreement that we are going to act in the other's best interest, then I can say that it is our moral responsibility to fulfil our potential. Or I can put it another way and say it is our moral endeavour to realise our full potential for the benefit of others.

Jack   And ourselves. That I completely agree with. I think that's what I've just been writing.

Jean   What have you been writing, Jack?

Jack   I was relating to that in a seminar that I attended here recently, when Cyril Selmes gave a talk on a world ethic. It was lovely, because he put together this amazing contradiction between the values that we're now saying we subscribe to and what would be the state of the reality of the world that we live in: children dying of starvation, the number of wars going on. There was just this amazing feeling of contradiction between the values we have said we strive to uphold and the social order that we are actually in. What seems to be the reality.

Jean   Did he simply describe the reality as it was or did he make a proposal how to ...

Jack   It was a review, whereby he was talking on a world ethic. This is what we were trying to work out, how to resolve the contradiction. That's why I think the work that you're doing is so important in a really practical way of taking those values, recognising the contradictions, and then all the time struggling to realise the values more fully. There's a difference here between the effort we're making and the kind of effort that was made by, say, the New Romantics of the 1970s.

Jean   Who were they?

Jack   There was a group of sociologists who were labelled 'The New Romantics', for whom everything appeared to be possible because it was in the imagination.

Jean   And this movement was labelled romantic. Again, the innocence that things can get better, is that it?

Jack   I think it was one of the criticisms that was levelled against them, that they had no understanding—or at least didn't demonstrate their understanding—about the pressures of the political forces that were actually working against the realisation of the vision they had. The point was that you must build in that understanding, otherwise the vision just remains a vision.

Jean I hope I've made that point sufficiently strongly in the manuscript. I've tried to show that action research as a way of doing things is practicable only if you take cognisance of the outer constraints. It's a point I didn't always acknowledge in my early days as an action researcher, but the experience of working in a public forum has certainly brought home the importance to me of recognising myself as a social being. I have to acknowledge the influence of others acting on me, as well as mine on them, and bow sometimes to the prevailing wind.

Becoming an action researcher in name is easy. Becoming one in deed is not. Calling myself an action researcher means that I subscribe to a form of discourse in which action research is spoken about. Being an action researcher means that I subscribe to an attitude which shapes the way that I live.

In my own beliefs, I can draw a parallel here between undertaking action research, and prayer. I think that similar sets of values underlie both endeavours. For many Christians, the idea of prayer means doing a specific thing, performing in a certain way; for some it may become a ritual. My own view is that prayer is something which I do all the time; I live in a way that puts me in touch with God. I am in touch through trying to live out my values in my life, and not only talking about them in a ritualistic sense.

My action research mentality means that I am open to all things new. In terms of my professional development, it means that I see my current state as a point from which I may progress. I never have a view of a 'closed' practice, of having reached a state in which I know all the answers. I may feel quite pleased (or not) with where I am, but I always acknowledge that the time will come soon to move on and push back the frontiers again.

Having said this, the first question that I need to ask is this:

1. Where do I start?

In Chapter 3 we saw that there are various schemes available to help individuals get started on their enquiries. I have suggested throughout that it is contrary to the spirit of action research to offer a particular model as a 'true' way of doing things, for fear this might lead to action research being seen as a technology rather than an attitude. It is up to the individual practitioner to survey the field and decide what is best for her own particular situation.

What I would suggest, however, is that it is possible to specify certain conditions in which action research may flourish, and to point out that, as potential action researchers, we need initially to assess where we are before we embark on a particular project.

In response to the question 'Where do I start?' I would say that it is important realistically to assess the situation in which the proposed project is located, and the reasons for embarking on it. Both these factors will contribute to the success of the enquiry, for they link together the environment (the energies operating from outside in) and the practitioner (the energies operating from inside out). They will also frame the form of the research question and its emphasis. Consider, for example, the questions:

What do I want to change?
Why do I want to change it?
How can I change it?

'What do I want to change?' suggests that I want to investigate something to do with the interaction between me and my environment. 'Why do I want to change it?' suggests that I am reflecting on my own reasons for action. 'How can I change it?' suggests that I have made a commitment to the need for change, and my own reasons for action, with the practical intent of involving myself as an agent in negotiating the relationship between me and my environment.

A realistic assessment of the location of the intended project will tell me if I ought to embark on it, and how much a chance of success it stands if I do. I have to ask questions like:

— can I realistically expect to bring about change here?
— will my colleagues be sympathetic to my initiatives?
— will I be able to persuade them to support me?
— will I be able to carry out my enquiry within the political/ economic constraints of my situation?
— will I have someone to help me, listen to me, comfort me when I do not know what to do next?

These are big questions, and they need sensitive consideration. We all admire people who challenge the larger system of which they are a part. Sometimes, however, the environmental constraints in which action research enquiries are located may lead practitioners to feel that they are banging their heads against a brick wall; and it can then be wisest to find a softer wall.

Such a decision, however, will depend on the enquirer's answer to the question 'Why do I want to change it?' If I am undertaking my enquiry for reasons of getting on in the world—the 'technical' aspect of human interests (see Habermas, 1972, and below)—I may continue it for as long as the cultural location is comfortable for me. If I am undertaking my enquiry for reasons of understanding and explaining the world—the 'rational' aspect of human interests—I will veer the focus of the enquiry so that possibly it adopts a different form, and may continue in this new form. If I am undertaking my enquiry for reasons of asking questions about the nature of the relationship between me and the environment—the emancipatory aspect of human interests—I can regard my enquiry as the process of finding and asking the right questions that will enable it to continue. I am not here aiming to bring about substantial changes in the world, so much as invite people to consider that there are other ways of doing things, other songs to sing; and that success here will result in changing the world. This third aspect can often include the first two, for it embraces the ideas of self-interest (self-aggrandisement, ambition, self-esteem), and self-realisation (effecting change in respect of the 'good order'). The emancipatory aspect enables me to question the nature of the relationship between these two aspects.

Some writers (for example, Carr and Kemmis, 1986) have suggested that action research may be used in technical, rational and emancipatory senses. I would say that it is the emancipatory element that offers the most educational way forward. For if I may find my own questions which will invite colleagues to respond by asking their own questions, I may say that I have improved the process of education for myself and for the people in my care.

If I then go on to ask 'How can I change it?' I am embarking on a specific action plan as the realisation of the questions I have considered. My action plan begins with assessing the situation that I want to change and proceeding, through trial and error, to bringing about change (see above, Chapter 3).

I want briefly to dwell on the starting point of an action plan. There is often an assumption that a problematic situation means that the enquirer sees a problem. I think this is a mistaken association in language that most of us make. For a situation to be problematic it needs to be in a state of readiness for change—not fixed, reified, static or closed. It needs to be inherently volatile. If a situation is non-problematic it has no potential for transformation. So when I say that my practice is problematic, I do not mean necessarily that it is beset with difficulties; I mean that it is interesting because it has the potential for further development. The aspect on which I focus may indeed be a problem, but it may equally well be a cause for celebration.

I think what I am saying here also indicates the enormous progress that has taken place within the action research movement, itself a cultural phenomenon that is in process of constant development. In the early days, when action research was emerging as a backlash to the imposition of technical forms of knowledge, and when the emphasis was on the promotion of the image of teacher as researcher, there was an understandable drive towards an identification of, and solution of practical workplace problems. That emphasis is clearly still current; but I think there is a new spotlight which is beginning to light up the stage of recognised good practice as an interesting forum for the study of how and why it may be transformed into better versions of itself. Action research is becoming a powerful means of celebrating the realisation of the good.

My personal response to the question 'Where do I start?' is articulated in Chapter 2; in terms of my personal and professional life, what do I know? By asking this question, I acknowledge myself as an active knower, and I responsibly assess my own strengths, as well as my weaknesses, to see how best I may use them in the service of myself and of others.

2. What are the locations in which I may do action research?

I have implied throughout that professionals are people who are working with others in life situations which need responsible management. One of the characteristics of professionals is that they influence the lives of other people, even to the point of managing their lives for them. Professionals not only have technical mastery of their subject—parenting, social care, commerce—but also have interpersonal mastery—communication, establishing educative relationships.

Action research, I have said, is a way of bringing about personal and professional development. The location in which action research takes place is the workplace—the home, the shop, the office. The conditions in which action research flourishes are those in which warm, caring relationships provide an atmosphere in which the democratic ideals of individuals' freedom, integrity and mutual respect may be realised. While recognising that these ideal situations are not realisable in many practical social situations (the background to the question 'What do I want to change? What characteristics of this situation need attention?'), action researchers are not so easily put off because they share a sense of vision that things can be changed and that they are able to change them *because of* and *through* that shared sense of vision ('Why do I want to change it? What are my reasons for wanting to take action?') So, while recognising the limitations of their current influence at the macro-level, they resolve to engage in communicative discourse at the micro-level ('How do I want to change it? What is my action plan?'), with a view to taking one step at a time, each step firmer because it evolved out of the previous one.

Whereas the location of action research may be the workplace, the location of the support is often removed from the workplace. In my view, this is a highly problematic issue which again brings into focus the epistemological foundation of action research and the nature of the educative relationships in which action research is practised. For if we regard action research as a thing that you do, then it is legitimate to expect practitioners to go to an institution in which action research is taught as a subject, to learn about its principles and practices, and go back to their own workplace and apply what they have learnt to themselves. If, on the other hand, we regard action research as a working orientation for the things we are doing anyway, only that, because of our action research approach we want to change the way we do them, then only learning about action research is inappropriate. What we then need is someone to help us cope with our present attitude and learn ourselves to develop it. Action research should not only be practitioner-centred but also practitioner's workplace-based.

This in turn depends on whether we are adopting an action research approach with a view to enhancing the quality of our own personal and professional development, or whether we are aiming for a formal accreditation to add to our professional portfolio (why do I want to change things?) Colleagues with whom I work often express a certain irritation when they are following through a particular enquiry and enjoying the new ideas and exciting outcomes, only to feel that they have to stop in mid-stream, and write it up for a report or dissertation. This can be highly frustrating, because of the sense of time-wasting involved in analysing and synthesising the data. Although I sympathise greatly here (constantly being aware myself of the rich moments of active life in the world that are gone forever), I do fully endorse the need for quiet times of active reflection, rigorous synthesis. It is often through hard thinking that we come to understand how and why we are dealing with the diversity of our relationships with others. I believe in the value of writing up the project, even though it may be conducted in a very informal sense; for writing, or externalising in other symbolic form, gives us access to our latent thoughts (McNiff, 1990). I believe also in adhering to the discipline of writing up to a particular professional brief, for this puts our work within the professional context of the public domain, where it may be critiqued, adopted or adapted, and will possibly influence the lives of those who read it.

Support mechanisms, then, are crucial. The current action research political map in the U.K. shows that the most usual location for support is in Higher Education. Favoured strategy is that professionals go to the institute to discuss their workplace practice with an institution-designated supporter. There are clear signs, however, that this format is changing, and the change, I feel, is being hastened by the market-orientation that has come into all sectors of education and, for this particular issue, into Higher Education. Institutes of Higher Education are addressing the problem of their own survival in terms of the number of clients they can attract. Increasing numbers of Higher Education institutions are recognising the difficulties involved in offering only Institution/University based courses, and are developing flexible-learning strategies, such as modular and distance-learning schemes, whereby practitioners may work towards accreditation within the workplace. It is quite clear that the days of teacher secondments as the main form of INSET have gone. Local financial management usually says that people stay at home and work for the good of the institution that pays them. This is usually so across the professions. Granted that short-stab courses are still available, most programmes of professional development are now conducted within, and for the benefit of, the workplace.

This has enormous implications for the role of practitioners within Higher Education. It also has implications for the managers across the professions. For Higher Education, colleagues have to take on board the challenge to their own status as 'professional knowers', in that they have to devolve the power of knowledge to the people that they are supporting. This in itself means that they have to re-assess their own conceptualisation of what constitutes a legitimate form of knowledge. Their social role needs radical overhaul, in that they have to regard themselves primarily as facilitators, and engage in educative relationships that will help practitioners to understand both their own, and their supporters', practice. There is no longer any room for a Higher Education hidden agenda that aims to establish a secret power base within the client's own institutionalised workplace. The relationship must be open and free, honest in deed as well as in word. As Higher Education consultants, we have to declare our intent to engage in the learning exercise with the practitioner whom we are supporting.

Further, managers within the professions have to do the same. At the moment there is much talk of partnerships, but, at the risk of seeming cynical, I wonder how many of these are paper partnerships rather than practical ones. If managers across the professions employ the services of Higher Education consultants to facilitate the personal and professional development of practitioners, those managers themselves must be part of the learning exercise as well. It is just no good setting oneself apart from the workforce and still hope to effect institutional development of the educational kind. The whole notion of an educative culture collapses as soon as one party steps out of the insider culture of self-reflective practitioners, and sets him or herself up in the abstracted outsider role of arranging for others to be educated.

I would also endorse the idea of partnership as acting in a cross-fertilisation programme whereby managers in the professions educate themselves, initially perhaps with the support of Higher Education, to become the professional educators within their own field. It seems to me that, unless managers take on this responsibility, the professional development of the practitioners for whom they are responsible will remain at the level of technical excellence rather than personal improvement.

At the moment, action research is alive and well in most departments of education within Higher Education. Many policy-making and funding bodies within the teaching profession have taken it on as a powerful approach to the professional learning of teachers (for example, Avon LEA). Many Institutions within Higher Education are offering practitioner-based distance-learning programmes to teachers, usually in the form of award-bearing courses. Many professions are running programmes in collaboration with Higher Education for the on-going professional learning of practitioners (see, for example, Elliott, 1989).

I am saying that now we need to re-draw the lines. Within the teaching profession, action research has brought about a re-definition of educational theory: from being grounded in the separate disciplines of education, we now have a 'living educational theory ' (Whitehead, 1989b), which has its base in the real lives of real people as they try to realise their educational values through the way they live.

We now need a new form of theory for the continuing professional development of practitioners at work. We need to abandon a view of professional knowledge as being vested in a tradition of line-management.

We need to encourage a view of professionals' learning as an exercise of communicative competence whereby we aim to air and share the values we hold as professionals in order to improve the quality of life for ourselves and for our fellows.

I do not yet know what to suggest in terms of a general Council to promote this view. Certainly I support the idea of a General Teaching Council to be responsible for the professional development of teachers. The GTC could take upon itself the responsibility for the professional learning of adults at work; I have argued that professional development is in fact conceptually linked with continuing education. The professional is grounded within the personal. However, I would like to expand a view of professional development outside the remit of the proposed GTC. My tentative thinking is that perhaps this would constitute part of the overall brief of a national council for adult and continuing education. As the current legislation bites, so trends will emerge that will signal the development of such initiatives.

In conclusion, then, let me say that my own view of how one becomes an action researcher is to look at both the inner and the outer perspectives of personal practice, and the dynamic relationship between the two. In terms of the inner perspective, I need to consider the particular issues I wish to address with reference to my work, and the form of the questions I will ask in order to address them. In terms of the outer perspective, I need to consider the social situation of which my work and my proposed project are a part, and decide if it is viable in terms of the external constraints that are potentially in operation. In particular, however, I need to ask myself about how I can link the two perspectives. I need to consider the relationship operating between me and my environment; to be honest with myself in terms of why I want to undertake my enquiry in the first place; and to consider the fact that I will probably have to compromise with others for my project to take place at all.

I think these sorts of considerations should be central within the action research literature, as well as case studies that show how people addressed them in real life; and I would recommend them to colleagues as of urgent concern when we are considering our own future as practitioners, or when, as managers of programmes of professional development, we are encouraging practitioners to become action researchers. For we cannot glibly say that we are going to become action researchers without accepting all the implications. Attempting to bring about a transformation of practice through personal commitment is potentially hazardous; and we must have our eyes well open before we leap.

Chapter Five

Implications and Critical Issues

Jean *It's really important to carry the idea of critique into the language we use. Just now we were talking about the meaning of 'freedom'. I said freedom holds within itself the notion of self-discipline.*

Jack *I don't think freedom has that. Justice has. I don't see that freedom has got that within it.*

Jean *Self-discipline. I think freedom of itself holds the idea of discipline.*

Moira *Otherwise it's licence. It has to be a disciplined exercise.*

Jean *It's not taking liberties.*

Jack *You say it's not taking liberties. My understanding is that freedom is taking liberties. Could we check freedom with other values? Are you trying to make the value of freedom do too much? Are you trying to bring into it other values which we've got to weigh against freedom, such as understanding, justice, care? But freedom usually means this notion of 'freedom to do something', or 'freedom from constraint' which is that notion of opposites in thinking about freedom. I've never associated freedom with checks within itself. If you are free it's very awesome.*

Jean *I am suddenly acutely aware how our whole language is a personal thing and yet it is a social activity. It has got to be a social interchange. As you were saying that, I'm reflecting on how it is that I come to use the word 'freedom' in that sense—my own use of the word reflects my experience of life which has made me use it in that sense. I can fully accept what you are saying there. My use of the word 'freedom' incorporates the values that I have explored in my own life to cause me to come to use the word in the way that I do. Yet, as you were speaking there, I was aware that my use of 'freedom' may not be the same as somebody else's. In spite of my talk of deconstruction, here I am reconstructing my own language, and overstepping normative boundaries.*

Jack   It might be useful to refer to your text where we will perhaps understand better, by using the term, not just through the language we use, but by examining our own practices. This is what I am trying to do in the text that I am working on at the moment, how I show my commitment to the values of freedom—in this case, academic freedom. Now, the meaning that I give to the term is clearer from going through the text. So maybe your text is really getting to what you would wish it to be. Are you showing in real contexts ways in which the fundamental values and also the spiritual dimension is being expressed, is being more fully lived? That's what I want to find out.

In this chapter I shall draw on the work that is being done in the field of education, again with the comment that this view may be generalised to other fields and professions. I want to look at some of the implications inherent in what has gone before, and to tackle some of the critical issues that are high in current action research thinking.

1. WHAT COUNTS AS ACTION RESEARCH?

There is a strongly shared view in the community of educational researchers that action research is a form of research that has evolved as an alternative to traditional forms. In traditional forms, advice was offered to teachers about how best to apply other researchers' findings to their own teaching.

In terms of educational theory, as it was applied to the work of teachers, the assumption was that practitioners could study the disciplines of education (philosophy, psychology, history, sociology, management) and use this public knowledge to improve what they were doing. This view was particularly endorsed in the 1960s and 1970s by the work of Professors Peters and Hirst of the London Institute. This trend in teacher education is parallel to the trends in other schemes of professionals' development (see, for example, Elliott, 1989) where practitioners operated within specific categories of knowledge to improve their performance. Action research now offers an opportunity to practitioners to abandon this dependency on traditional forms of knowledge and professional development, and trust their own latent ability that they already have the answers to improvement in their own hands. What they do need, in terms of support, is the encouragement to make that knowledge explicit and have it validated within the public domain.

As I have pointed out, there are differences of opinion about the underlying values that the authors of specific approaches hold that cause them to promote the views that they do. Where there is solid agreement among the community, however, is in the fact that action research needs to be made public (shared) and that it has to meet rigorous criteria that indicate that it is scientific research. Again let me stress that these criteria are not applicable only within the teaching profession: they are criteria applicable to research programmes, no matter what the field is in which the programme is carried out.

Altrichter *et al* (1991) have also pointed out the danger in trying too hard to aim for a concrete definition of action research, and they offer working criteria that qualify an enquiry as operating in an action research mode. They agree that an action research approach may be recognised in terms of certain characteristics: "The general aims of action research are frequently expressed in terms of orienting process criteria (e.g. participation, emancipation) rather than in the form of objectives to be achieved, and it seems worthwhile to continue to stress the characteristics to differentiate action research from other approaches to social change. At the same time it should be acknowledged that we have not yet reached the end of the development of action research. ... we must avoid behaving as if doing action research were no more than administering a defined strategy. This developmental orientation lies at the very heart of action research and every definition must do justice to this orientation."

They offer a 'working characterisation' of action research. They suggest that mine may be a situation in which action research may be occurring if it provides an environment in which people may (a) share insights of experience, and aim for improvement through action-reflection; (b) engage in individual and collective data-gathering, analysis and synthesis, and work towards establishing a critical community; (c) continue to explore new elements in a spirit of open enquiry.

As an action researcher I find this kind of approach helpful, in that it offers me an imagined scenario of what things might look like if I undertake my own action enquiry. It tells me not what to do so much as the sort of conditions I need to look for to help my project to succeed. As a form of educational theory that will help me to improve my own practice, however, it fails me in the sense that here again is a theory which I have to apply. I get no sense of how the authors themselves have brought about the improvement in their own social situation as they are recommending that I do through following their advice. It simply is not enough, in order to advance a form of theory that has implications for the living practice of real people, to offer theory in the conceptual form of paper theory, without showing the demonstration of the living proof that acts as evidence for the advertisement. Whitehead (1992), in response to Zuber-Skerrit (1991), makes the same point:

"I am proposing that educational theory is ... being constituted by the descriptions and explanations which individual learners are producing for their educational development in enquiries of the kind, 'How do I improve my practice?' ... I suppose the main challenge to academics in the above views is the implication that their research should include a public account of their own educational development in an enquiry of the form, 'How do I improve my practice?' To hold oneself accountable in this way, in the name of education and one's own humanity, may deter those who prefer the safety of conceptual structures. There is risk, a creative leap and an act of faith, involved in attempting to make original contributions to educational knowledge."

In considering my own view as to what counts as one of the critical issues facing action research, I would respond that we need evidence as much as rhetoric. Papers embodying conceptual forms of theory that articulate the nature of action research are not themselves evidence of action research if they do not offer the internal justification of how they constitute part of the improvement of living practice. For me, what counts as action research is living evidence, a living theory, that shows the improvement of the quality of a life, as it is lived, in a spirit of enquiry and openness towards life and all that it offers.

2. WHAT IS THE NATURE OF EDUCATIONAL ACTION RESEARCH?

The word 'education' probably has so many meanings for so many people that it could often seem meaningless in itself. Certainly there is no standardised agreement about what 'education' or 'educational' *means*. I would hazard a guess, however, that those who are in education as a profession share a common values base, and this would include the desire for the welfare of clients, and the development of their knowledge. I am not so sure that there would be such agreement of the form that that knowledge would take. Many educationists show that they believe in the supremacy of objective knowledge (note the market orientation that has taken over educational endeavour in this country that produces an emphasis on the acquisition and perfection of skills). Action researchers see personal development as the general orientation in which professional development is grounded, and they focus initially on encouraging the living 'I' to improve her or himself.

Let me suggest that, in the context of this book, 'education' is taken to refer to the development of an individual's understanding, and 'educational' is the term used to describe aspects that concern that development. By implication, 'educational' may be applied to processes that aim for development, or improvement; the terms 'education', 'development' and 'improvement', while not synonymous, are conceptually related and are often used to infer parallel processes in normal language.

I now want to explore the nature of development, and here I must make a clear statement about my use of language. In normal language, 'development' may be taken to denote a process, in a value-free sense. I may talk about the development of sensitivity, for example, or the development of an illness. In the judgement of a rational society, sensitivity is deemed a positive aspect of a good order or system, whereas illness indicates a negative aspect of a good order or system. Consider that I aim to let my life constitute a good order, but the flu from which I am suffering mars it. Yet the flu itself is developing well in its own terms. In a social setting, a rational society might condemn the rise of dogmatic, destructive forces; in terms of that judgement, such success constitutes imbalance within the good order of the whole society, perhaps even dysfunction; but the evil forces within are progressing nicely. In this conceptualisation, 'development' may be considered in a value-free sense as a neutral process of moving forward.

In the following discussion I want to give the word 'development' value, to use it in the sense that it is a value-laden process to do with the realisation of potential. As such, I am relating the concepts of development and improvement. For a thing to develop, it has to metamorphose into a version of itself that is by definition better. If it metamorphosed into a version of itself that is worse, that process would be regression, or degeneration. Degenerative processes, while clearly processes of change, may hardly be termed processes of development. A process of development may be characterised as one that realises the inherent good order of the system of which the thing is a part.

Now let me relate the concepts of development and education. Education is a process whereby personal development is enhanced. (Note that I am using the word 'education' in that value-laden sense, and not talking about a neutral process). The implication I want to draw out is that there are categorical parallels between developmental processes and educational processes. This is an important conceptual link. When we are talking about schemes of professional development, we must also enter into a consideration of the continuing education of practitioners at work.

I think this is usually accepted within professional discourse when it is about the continuing education of teachers. I do not think it is such common currency when the discourse is about continuing education within other professions.

Let me link this now with the idea of action research as educational, and I will draw two conclusions.

1. Action research in itself has to be educational—that is, it has to engage in processes that lead to a realisation of the good. In my view, educational research is itself a moral enterprise. By 'moral' I understand that you and I act in the best interest of the other so that each one of us, as a living 'I', may realise his or her own potential, for the intended benefit of the other. By 'moral enterprise' I understand that we as individuals are all part of processes that operate as part of an existing culture, but that we exercise our individuality to help that culture to develop (improve). Lest I be accused of naivety, let me say that I believe that cultural processes, and all their social, political, economic and historical concomitants, evolve out of the practical intentions of two or more individuals acting within a common relational framework. It is the practical intent of those individuals for the other that will determine their immediate view of how they will deal with their environment. The evolution of a rational society rests on such commitments—the practical intent of caring individuals to improve the quality of life for themselves and others.

Jack Whitehead has this to say:

"I want to make a distinction between action research and educational action research in terms of values. If action research is characterised by a particular form of systematic enquiry then there is no necessity to justify the value base of the enquiry in defining the research as 'action research'. Action research could, in these terms, be used to increase the efficiency of activities which could be morally unacceptable. In claiming that my research is 'educational' I am not willing to accept the term 'educational' to describe activities which are undermining these values." (Whitehead, 1990).

2. I believe that continuing professional education is not the prerogative only of those within the profession of education. I believe that it ought to be part of the remit of the professions themselves to take on the responsibility for the continuing education of the practitioners within that profession. To some extent this is already happening, but, in my opinion, it is not happening enough. There is also some slippage in what counts as legitimate professional knowledge, and more emphasis needs to be placed on the idea of professional development in the workplace. At the moment, the 'location of knowledge' seems to be within the Higher Education sector. I pointed out before that the hi-jacking by academics of action research as a way to characterise their own work as teacher educators had secured a place for action research as a legitimate form of professional activity. I think the view of Higher Education as the 'location of knowledge' is being endorsed by the professions who apply to institutes of education to conduct programmes of professional development for their own practitioners. It is also being endorsed by those in institutes of Higher Education who regard themselves as knowers, rather than learners.

I think the scenario in Britain is changing substantially and rapidly from what I have described above. There are increasingly frequent signs that professional relationships are developing between Higher Education and the professions that operate in a sense of collegiality—a true partnership in deed as well as in word—that emphasises the sharing of knowledge itself as a creative enterprise. This view needs to be disseminated much more vigorously, however; and, in my opinion, there needs to be a redefinition of the educational political scenario and a restructuring of the power relations at work in the legitimation of professionals' educational knowledge. I think incumbents in Higher

Education, who are by their position legitimised as 'professional knowers', need actively to share their control of knowledge by involving themselves in national accreditation schemes that legitimise the educational knowledge of professionals at work. I also think the incumbents themselves should undertake their own educational enquiries into their own personal and professional development, and make those findings public (see below, part 2). Let me stress also that what I am suggesting in terms of continuing professional education is not a plea for provision for further technical training. It is the articulation of my sense of vision that continuing education should be the entitlement of all professionals at work; and that programmes of personal and professional development are not abstracted from normal life, such that individuals have to go to an institution which is deemed the 'location of knowledge'. Instead, individual professionals should be encouraged to undertake their own personal enquiries, supported by educators within their own profession, and within their own workplace, to improve the quality of education for themselves and for each other. I am not denying the prerogative of Higher Education to award degrees; but I am suggesting that the status of in-house education schemes should be enhanced such that experience gained through such schemes should be recognised as falling within the Higher Education AP(E)L remit; and that such a trend should be systematically incorporated into current structures of Credit Accumulation and Transfer.

In Section 4 I will speak to the 'professional educators', and discuss the nature of the power base within educative relationships that will improve the quality of education for all the participants in the enterprise. To lead in to that issue, I now want to look at the idea of collaborative action research, how it works, and how it is taking the whole action research movement forward.

3. HOW DO WE MOVE FROM 'I' TO 'WE'?

The notional mechanics of collaborative action research are these:

An individual undertakes her own enquiry to see if she can improve a particular aspect of her work. She carries through a systematic programme of identification of problems—imagined solutions—implementation of solutions—evaluation of solutions—modification of actions and ideas in the light of the evaluation. She aims to make a claim to knowledge: that is, to say that she *knows*—in this instance, that she knows she has brought about improvement within the particular situation that she has been focusing on. She has to demonstrate the validity of that claim: that she is not just making it up, but that she has evidence to show its inherent truth. For this she needs to point to the data and offer it for other people's judgement, so that they may say that improvement actually has occurred or not.

In claims to knowledge which are empiric in nature—that rest on public, objectified knowledge—I can point to concrete evidence to support that claim. I know that this is a pen because here it is in my hand. I know that today is Friday because it says so on my newspaper. In claims to knowledge that are subjective in nature—that rest on my own private knowledge—I have to ask you to validate what I am saying. I feel that something is so because I can point to something out of my own experience. I ask you to support my claim. Together we have to work out criteria within the situation that I hope to affect, that we both believe are indicative of aspects that I am focusing on; and together we have to trace those aspects, as they are realised in action, through the process of the enquiry to show that those aspects do in fact change, and that they change for the better.

For example, as a dentist's receptionist, I am trying to improve the quality of life for the patients in the waiting room. I am unhappy about the physical surroundings. The waiting room is drab and uninteresting. I decide to do something about it. I explain to the dentists in the partnership that I feel we could improve things, and they agree that life must be pretty grim for the patients. I tell my receptionist colleagues as well, and they agree that the surroundings do seem to affect the disposition of the patients: children get fractious (there are no toys or other play resources), parents get bored and nervous (there are no decent magazines), some patients get nervous and gloomy (the stained wallpaper and cracked paint do not communicate an atmosphere of good cheer). Furthermore, patients are actively heard to grumble: "What a miserable place this is. Bad enough you come to have your teeth done without walking into a morgue as well."

We feel that brightening up the surroundings will improve matters, and, with the support of the partners and my receptionist colleagues, I arrange to have the waiting room redecorated in a bright, sunny colour; I purchase flowers for the desk and window sill; I organise a play area for the children with toys and appropriate reading matter; I arrange for a supply of clean, up-to-date magazines; I arrange for light, cheerful music to be piped through. My colleagues and I agree that things are much better. So do the patients. Over time they are heard to say, "Isn't this nice! The children love coming here just to play with the games. And I don't mind it a bit—nice cheerful place to be in. At least you don't think about having your teeth done all the time."

At the same time, to boost the economic viability of the business, I place advertisements in the local press. 'Tooth problem?' goes the legend. 'Come to I. Pullum and partners, dental surgeons. New improved facilities. Latest technology.' I then insert a small paragraph from a conversation with a patient, saying how relaxed and confident she feels when she comes to the surgery, and how she urges others to do the same for the benefit of their oral health.

So successful does the business become that the partners decide to put my name forward for the Molar Award as receptionist of the year (as well as giving me a nice bonus). The story is picked up by Ian Wright, a handsome young reporter, and it is recorded in the 'Dentists' Monthly'. Snippets from interviews with me, the partners, patients, and other receptionists are included in the report. While he is working on the story, we fall in love, Ian asks me to marry him and we live happily ever after.

This action research fairy story has all the elements of a personal enquiry which has the potential for a collaborative enquiry but doesn't quite fulfil the potential. The elements it contains for an individual's personal enquiry are that (a) the individual planned a systematic enquiry how to improve something; (b) carried out that enquiry actually to effect improvement; (c) demonstrated that she had improved matters, thus enabling her to make a claim to educational knowledge; (d) told others what she was doing and involved them in working through the enquiry with her, thus making her enquiry public; (e) involved them in identifying criteria (elements of practice) to show what needed improving and how it was improved; (f) demonstrated that they shared opinion that things had improved, thus justifying her claim to educational knowledge.

It would be easy to extend this enquiry into the community and make it truly a collaborative enquiry. Let's imagine that my actions inspired a colleague in another dentists' practice to do the same as I did. She, however, wanted to improve the quality of the aftercare of the patients as they came out of surgery. She planned, in company with her colleagues, that they should set up a small recovery room where patients could sit or lie down for a while, have a cup of tea, telephone someone to talk through their experience. She enlisted the help of the health service to provide a nurse.

Throughout our separate projects, she and I compared notes. We met frequently, listening to each other, suggesting how we might separately refine our enquiries, and borrowing ideas from each other. We formed a partnership, in that we supported each other emotionally and intellectually.

She and I decided to share our research with colleagues at our professional education centre, and the leader there arranged for us to give a talk to nurses attending a training course. In sharing our separate enquiries with each other, and then later with our colleagues, we turned what started as an individual's enquiry into a collaborative, shared enquiry. The epistemic centre of the enquiry remained the living 'I'—I explored my own practice—but the methodological focus transformed 'I' into 'we'—we communicated to each other our own developed understanding, and established a culture of intersubjective agreement.

There are a number of case studies in the literature where this transformation is evident (for example, Lomax, 1989, 1991; McNiff, 1992. In this text you are reading I have attempted to demonstrate the transformation from individual to collaborative enquiries.) Practitioners tell their own stories of how they improved the quality of education for themselves and for others. There are many issues here that need to be addressed, not least the political aspects to do with role and self-esteem. As Pamela Lomax says: 'Involving all colleagues and perhaps forming a critical community of staff that uses action research as the basis for personal and institutional development is an ideal that is difficult to achieve. Some colleagues will be reluctant to be involved. This raises ethical issues as well as a need for the action researcher to safeguard his or her own professional role.' (Lomax, 1991)

I think this aspect is fundamental to the continuance of action research as a legitimate form of educational research. Far from becoming an orthodoxy, as some researchers claim, I think action research is highly vulnerable to the challenge that it is a self-indulgent pastime which assumes, as did Candide, that we all live in a best possible world that we can adapt as we will (see, for example, Adelman, in Carr, 1989).

Let me then look at this very important issue, and suggest that currently this is the most significant hurdle that we need to negotiate in order for the movement itself to survive as a way of looking at things. For unless we take a long hard look at the nature of the educative relationships of which we are a living part, action research is in danger of becoming just another discipline that we can study as an abstraction instead of providing an attitudinal orientation for the way that we live our lives.

4. THE NATURE OF EDUCATIVE RELATIONSHIPS

Many human relationships are grounded in power. Power may take many forms—authority, wealth, status, fitness, age, gender, race, creed, and so on. The person who is agreed to be in power is seen by all participants in the relationship as the holder of the power-base. In a relationship that takes wealth as the sign of power, she who has the wealth is the most powerful. In a relationship where physical strength is the sign of power, she who is strongest is also the most powerful. And in a relationship where knowledge is the sign of power, she who knows is the most powerful.

We need to return to the issue that there are different kinds of knowledge. If we take the view that public, objectifiable knowledge is the legitimate form of knowledge, this will reinforce the idea that in a 'knowing' relationship there is a knower and an aspirant knower. This is, I believe, the relationship that is most common in many fields of education, including that of professional development. In the line-management model discussed earlier, there is an insidious view that the manager knows best and is therefore authorised to control the efforts of the practitioner. This view is also apparent in traditional forms of research, where an 'outsider' researcher does research on 'insiders'. It is assumed that, because the outsider knows (usually in the sense that she is armed with theory) she may make judgements about the practitioner and require him to come up to her standard. Even in well-intentioned schemes where the manager acts as an adviser, she still carries the stamp of authority, that she is more knowledgeable than the aspirant knower.

Now, I am not saying that technical knowledge about a subject is unnecessary. In my own work as a professional educator, I need to have acquired a lot of substantial knowledge about the subject which I need to communicate to colleagues. In this sense I have a specific body of public knowledge—I know-that certain things are so—and I have to pass this information on. It would be quite wrong of me not to help colleagues to acquire this knowledge in an efficient manner, so I provide all sorts of sign-posts for them to resources and information-bearing systems. In this way I am an efficient manager of substantial knowledge, of information.

What, though, of how I help my colleagues to come to know, to develop their own personal and professional knowledge? This is hardly a case of know-that, or even of know-how. It is a case of developing experience, and knowledge of that experience. It is a case of developing personal and professional wisdom. I cannot communicate that knowledge in any form other than by living it.

This is a hard concept to grasp, and an even harder thing to do. Truly to live out my values, I have to make a conscious commitment to those values. If I am saying, as an educator, that the development of professional knowledge lies in the willingness of the practitioner critically to look at her own work, I must start with myself. If I want to change something I have to become part of it, enter into it, and take it into myself. I cannot stand aside, look at it as an abstraction, and make pronouncements on how I feel it ought to be changed. I have to become part of the living system that I am wanting to influence, and accept at the same time that it is influencing me, in the same way as I hope I am influencing it. It cannot just be an object of study that I am observing and commenting on from a distance. It has to be a field of practice in which we all acknowledge that we are changing entities within the changing world. In my work as an educator, I cannot seek to change people and the systems of which they are a part unless I am willing first to be aware of how I change, how I change the world, and how it changes me.

This dialectical relationship is the basis for relationships that are educative. Education begins with the practitioner—it is the practitioners' own development of herself. Action research is the practitioner's own study of herself. It is not the practitioner's study of someone else.

The implications for programmes of professional development are that the manager of the programme has to commit herself to the idea that she is first focusing on her own self development, with a view to communicating the growth of her own understanding to her fellow practitioners, so that they may learn from and follow her example; and this attitude has a significant bearing on the question of power relationships. Power is not vested in any one person or any one role. The fact that I am manager of a learning situation does not mean that I already know the answers or the outcomes or the indicators that will show that learning has taken place. It means that I have already committed myself to the need to develop my own learning. If I did not hold this attitude, I would disqualify myself from being manager of the learning situation. Educators are primarily learners, not knowers. They openly acknowledge that their knowledge is never complete. It is always transforming, always growing. Martin Buber (1947) speaks of the humility of the educator, and I think that it is here that humility lies—in my acknowledgement that I still have far to go. This is not to say that I am ignorant. Far from it. In my professional role I hold a good deal of public knowledge, and my personal knowledge of my own potential and ability allows me to say with confidence that I know my own self, my own work. But through that very confidence I am able openly to acknowledge that my fund of knowledge never will be complete. I enjoy the process always of enlarging upon my own knowledge. It is fun, exciting, constantly pushing back the frontiers.

My commitment to on-going evaluation of my work in order to get to know that work better is part of an action research approach, constantly trying out new solutions to ever-emerging potentially problematic situations. The relationship between individuals who are all committed to this view is not grounded in power structures, but in the trust of the one for the other to improve the quality of life for self and others. If I am a manager of the learning situation I acknowledge this—that we are all working in the other's best interest. I am not worried about power over someone else, either as a means or an end. This kind of power is not even part of my repertoire. I acknowledge no barriers between you and me because none exist in a truly educative relationship.

In terms of current forms of professionals' learning, what this implies is networking instead of the hierarchical structures of management, drip-feed, cascade, or whatever name we care to give to the model. In fact, the idea of model almost becomes redundant, for we are no longer looking at analogies that characterise 'ways to do things'. This is what I have indicated throughout, that the term 'action research' is a metaphor of which there are a growing number of examples. A 'model', for me, implies a structure, a 'way' as a 'thing'. I regard concepts like 'action research' and 'networking' as concepts which embody certain values which are realised in and through the ongoing lives of real people. A network is a network because it is alive. A model somehow exists on a piece of paper. A model is an abstraction. It is only in its real application within the real world that the model takes on meaning, in and through you and me. We are action researchers because we adopt an open, questioning frame of mind, because we are open to our own sense of process, because it is our practical intent to improve the quality of our own lives for the sake of others. Any relationship that we enter into has to be educative, because we abdicate notions of power in our honest attempt to improve the quality of life. Our humility is not self-effacing. It is the quiet, responsible commitment by self-reflective practitioners to understand the world from their own point of view, to make that knowledge explicit, and thus to enable others to do the same thing if they wish.

As I said at the beginning, there is no such thing as action research, but there are definitely things called action researchers. It is my firm belief that their contribution will make the world a better place.

Jean   Going back to Moira's point about the nature of the educative relationship, you have to take on the responsibility of empowering people to disagree with you. You have to take on that responsibility with very wide open eyes, because unless you're prepared to accept the consequences you don't enter the game. Once you do enter the game, once you do make that commitment to lower the drawbridge and let other people in to what until now has been unassailable integrity, and you lay yourself open, unless you are prepared to take on that responsibility you just don't do it, because it can inflict quite terrible wounds on you, and unless you have the personal strength to combat it you have to be careful. This I think is a fundamental aspect of working as an educator.

Moira   But the recognition that others may abuse your integrity is your strength. If someone does that to me, I feel that something about the educative relationship has been successful, so in that sense I'm not abused at all. I feel that in some ways I'm in the profession as an educator because I want in that sense to become obsolete. Therefore it's almost necessary for them to reject. That it seems is wholly healthy, and therefore it cannot wound me. It is those people who are unable to do that who are then perhaps the ones who I should be concerned about. What are you smiling about, Jack?

Jack   There's a nice tension here. I agree with what you are saying, but in practice I am torn. Like when Peggy Kok wrote at the end of her dissertation: 'I had said explicitly that the value that underpins the form of the action research that I would take back with me [to Singapore] would be the value of excellence in performance.

It is at this point that I moved away in spirit from the living educational theory because, as I told Whitehead: the values that I bring back [are] not your values, but the values I have come to on my own.' (Kok, 1991) Now, I think that's really wonderful. It must be like this—you know, people leave you. On the one hand you wish them to be autonomous, and to leave, because they are autonomous; on the other hand you're faced—well, I feel this .. this kind of wrench.

Jean   It is the nature of life. It is the nature of change, that we converge and we part. When we part we take that bit of the other person that has added to our own growth. We take the other person with us in ourselves. So in that sense there is no parting, because we carry each other with us all the time.

PART TWO

THE GENERATIVE ORDER
OF EDUCATIONAL
KNOWLEDGE

Part Two:

The Generative Order of Educational Knowledge

23rd November, 1991

Scene: School of Education, University of Bath. The following people are assembled: Phil Coates, Kevin Eames, Mary Gurney, Terry Hewitt, Moira Laidlaw, Jean McNiff, Peter Mellett, Jack Whitehead. We are discussing the idea that the conversation we are holding and audiotape recording might be used as part of the work in progress.

Jean   What I'd really like to capture for the purposes of this text is this: I'd like to transcribe this conversation between us that shows our sense of community, and the way in which a community can evolve out of dialogue. Do you think that we have already stated sufficiently our sense of community, or would you wish something more substantial to be said about our statements and intent?

Kevin   Are you looking for a description?

Jean   I don't think so. I think I'm looking for some sense of unity through the values that we share, the evolutionary process.

Jack   Then I don't think what we've said so far is enough. Today has given me the opportunity to share something, to give something freely, and which we can celebrate. But I feel I still need to make the kinds of political statements about the economic and political conditions and influences which we as teachers and practitioners seem to be being subjected to, and in particular the whole ethos of those monetarist policies coming through in terms of the feeling that the way in which we're valued now is in terms of cash, and that the kind of values and ethics that we subscribe to are not being given high-value status within our community. So I don't think that just the celebration is enough. I think it's almost the feeling that all of you are strengthening me for action I actually believe in.

Mary   I'd like to ask that question again—I need to know what this group here means to each one of us, and how we take from the group and how we interact and so on. What the community is about. That's what I'm looking for.

So I went home, and transcribed the tape, and wondered what to do with the conversation, what to do now with the voices of my colleagues that were entrusted to my care. How should I portray them? How could I do justice to the richness of our dialogue, our lack of duplicity in working through emergent ideas with each other, present the whole in an edited form to a general readership without distorting the message or violating the integrity of my companions?

How could I stay true to myself and continue with the theme of the text, of presenting my own claim to knowledge through the book while using the book to critique that very claim? My claim is that I have improved my own education, and I have indicated as a substantial proposition within the text that making such a claim is a necessary step for action researchers to take—to demonstrate how and why they have improved. How could I continue to demonstrate that the book was a continuation of that theme, and yet use the book to test the claim that I was making?

I spent a long time thinking. I mentally rehearsed many routines of observing, imagining solutions, trying them out, evaluating them ... and then I sat down to write. As always with me, the writing itself offered the spur to creativity—and here is another example of self-reflexive spirals: for the act of writing generated new ideas, and the new ideas helped new writing to unfold. I decided to focus on the central theme of my own project—the idea of generativity—which I consider is fundamental to the very notion of a creative way of life; and see if I could test the idea against the reality of our dialogue, if I could refine my own ideas through our community process of theorising.

Here, then, is the result. When I have finished writing the text, I shall send it to the companions who were present on 23rd November, and ask them to comment. I hope their responses may be embodied in their own future texts, as well as mine, that will constitute part of my own project of promoting democratic forms of educational knowledge by encouraging people to speak with their own voices.

Chapter Six

Generativity, Reflective Practice and Self Explanation

I need to make the point that in this section I am speaking from my perspective as a teacher. Whereas until now I have talked about action research as being applicable to schemes of professional development in general, in this part I am approaching the argument via the work that is being done in education.

I want to focus on the idea of action research as a generative form of enquiry. It would probably be useful first to give a brief explanation of the concept of generativity, and to say how and why I have come to regard it as fundamental to human enquiry in general and educational enquiry in particular.

I must here make the same statement as before (page 53), that I am using the word 'generativity' in a value-laden sense, while acknowledging that it also has a normal language use in which it is used to denote a neutral process.

My first remembered encounter with the magic of generativity was when, as a child, I watched snowflakes settling on the window pane. I was captivated by the idea that the snowflake in its entirety seemed to consist of basically the same shape repeated in a symmetrical pattern. Although this observation was not accurate, the idea of generativity took hold: that it was possible for a basic form to generate itself infinitely, giving rise to a limitless number of new transformations, each transformation being an unfolding of the basic form that was enfolded within it from birth right through its transforming life. Subsequent study has introduced ideas of different kinds of order, of which I feel generative order is the most important.

I encountered the word 'generativity' when I read the work of Goethe during my undergraduate studies. I was fascinated by the way that he captured the idea of the power of potential encapsulated within a base unit. Goethe drew on his study of plants, and used the concept of 'Urpflanz' to present this idea: that is, the 'original plant', which, in his representation, was a prototype leaf. I do not think Goethe conceived of any one particular plant—just the idea of 'plant' as a basic form. Each and every plant was a manifestation of the 'Urpflanz' as it transformed itself through a process of minimal steps into its full-blown form.

Goethe extended the idea of generativity into the field of literature. His short story entitled 'Novelle' held within itself every characteristic necessary for a 'Roman', an extended work, or novel.

My interest in generativity was formalised further by my later reading of Chomsky, and his ideas of the generative transformational capacity of language. When I began my own research study I applied various aspects of Chomsky's thinking to my own work. I applied the idea of competence and performance to my understanding of personal development, and came to draw a parallel between Chomsky's ideas of levels of mind and the ideas of tacit and explicit knowledge (Polanyi, 1958: see McNiff, 1989). I considered a possible generative transformational approach to in-service support; this drew on the notion of action-reflection spirals which could provide a representation of an action-reflection approach to personal enquiry (McNiff, 1984). I have also applied the idea of Chomsky that a finite number of components can generate an infinite number of creative acts (Chomsky feels that a finite number of rules can generate a grammar, and consequently an infinite number of original utterances: Chomsky, 1986).

I am synthesising these ideas by considering the work of Bohm, of an enfolding and unfolding generative order as a reflection of an underlying unified reality (Bohm, 1983, 1987). I am applying these ideas in the synthesis of my current research interests, in investigating the generative transformational nature of communication. In this text, I am exploring how we might move our lives forward by tapping our potential for communicative competence through creating dialogical communities.

I am currently working on the issue of what educational theory would look like if seen as part of an unfolding generative order. Let me explain:

Following the ideas of Bohm, I understand that people imagine two basic views of order as representing the nature of reality: a linear order and a generative order. In the linear order, there is a notional progression in which singularities follow each other in a fixed sequence. A feature of such an order is that movement is one-directional: $A \longrightarrow B \longrightarrow C \longrightarrow n$. There is no going back, and no deviation from the normative direction. When the idea of development enters into the notion of the linear order, that development is seen in terms of structural change, in which B is different from A, usually by merit of additions to, or transformations of, the pre-existent structure. The field of stage-developmental theory is an example. This order is generally seen as permanent and unchanging, and, in my view, exists primarily as a conceptual form by which people try to organise their experience of reality in a functional way. My own view is that our cultural heritage encourages us to regard linear order as a readily available resource, and, such is its facile attractiveness, we tend to use it uncritically to help us make sense of all our realities.

A general tendency throughout the history of educational theory has been to regard it as existing as a subject mainly within the linear order. The task of educational research has been to accommodate new observations about the nature of educational practice within the general framework. This adaptation of new facts within reified structures is apparent in, for example, the general acceptance of empiric procedures as the most efficient way to predict and control professional development.

Within the framework of the unchanging order, the notion of educational theory takes the form of discrete and often competing bodies of reified knowledge. Changes in theory, from this point of view, become synapses, sharply defined transition points, in which the significant features of one set of givens are radically different from those of another. The task of educational research is to account for the changes, and offer descriptions and explanations for the emergence of the new bodies of knowledge which are frequently offered in the sense of discrediting what has gone before. The view of fragmentation is legitimated. Barriers are erected and demolished as the linear order marches on remorselessly, leaving a long trail of systematic refutation behind.

I want to suggest, following Bohm, that this general reliance on the idea of linear order is in fact a manifestation of a world view that constructs reality in terms of fragmentation. This view has profound implications for aspects of professional development, and for the study of such aspects. An outcome of a view of reality as fragmented is that the development of professional practice is a question of studying the established theory and adapting one's way of life to it. Another outcome is that the study of professional development is a question of reinforcing the reified conceptual form of educational theory by offering yet more variations on the theme within the same conceptual forms to saturate the market and persuade the consumers that quantity spells quality. Changes might take place in our views about educational theory but they are all still presented within the basic order or logic which itself does not appear to change.

An alternative view to this is to entertain the notion of a generative order, in which reality is represented as a seamless whole, in a constant process of unfolding. A view of the wholeness of the generative order does not entertain a view of educational theory as existing as a fixed structure. A state of constant coming into being cannot conceive of any form of finite structure or stasis, for the field is in universal flux and all experience is transformational. The idea of theory as an immutable body of knowledge becomes redundant, for theory, as are the thought structures of the person who creates the theory, is in a constant state of evolving into a different version of itself.

What would be a view of educational theory if we loosened our dependency on the idea of theory-as-structure, and sought rather to develop our insight and understanding without an end product in sight? What form would it take?

First, let me review the idea of what the reality might be like that underlies a particular view of order. Within the linear order it is convenient to suppose that the observer and the observed stand in opposition to each other. The observer performs various mental operations upon the object in order to take it into her knowledge system. Within the wholeness of the generative order there is no distinction between observer and observed, between knower and what is known, for everything is part of the overall pattern. A useful analogy would be to imagine a roll of fabric whose pattern comprises roses, lilies and ferns. Although it is possible to identify the separate elements as representing aspects of reality, the reality of the material is that the pattern exists as a continuum, and itself is realised as a continuous roll (see also Bohm, 1987). The meaning of the material is its unity. So it is with observer and observed. Each stands in a tension of unity, one unfolding with and through the other.

In terms of educational theory, the wholeness of the generative order offers a view of meaning as being embodied in the patterns of the lives of people as they strive to improve their understanding. Instead of the fragmented 'front end' view of theory guiding practice, we are asked to embrace a notion of the seamlessness of transforming insight as a continuous movement that itself may be characterised as theory. The educational nature of theory may be seen in the direction within the movement towards improvement—each notional transformation is a better version of the thing than it was before, and holds within itself the power to sustain an infinite number of improved and improving original transformations.

Educational theory within a linear order exists as a body of reified knowledge that may be applied to the lives of people in order to help them improve the quality of their understanding. For me, the premise on which this view stands is highly questionable, and arises from a view of reality as fragmented. I wonder whether individual or community understanding can be transformed by applying layers of theory, much as I have tried in my clumsy way to smarten up my house timber by applying several coats of paint. I have succeeded in executing a holding operation; but the underlying material is no different.

Educational theory within a generative order exists in the transforming understanding of real people as they try to give meaning to their lives. It is essentially a living process. Although it may be characterised in an abstract form, as demonstrated here, in my attempt to explain my understanding of the notion, that understanding itself is the form that the theory takes. This book is a manifestation of this idea. The group has shared its thoughts. By sharing these thoughts with you, through the written words which will transform themselves into our shared understanding, our separate lives diffuse into mutuality. We constitute our own theory, in terms of allowing the idea enfolded within our values system to unfold into the reality of our worldly actions. This continuous unfolding of the enfolded values gives a meaning to our lives.

In my project, I want to promote the popularity of a view of the generative order, of which a living educational theory is a part, as a more accurate representation of the reality that underlies our lives as educators. In my view, it is the commitment to the fragmentation of the linear order that keeps many of us in blinkered thrall. For we not only fail to see the possibility of other orders, other ways of life; we also fail to see that the idea of order, which humankind created as a functional tool in the first place, has overtaken us, and exists in an abstracted reified form external to our own consciousness. We have established the idea of linear order somehow as a force over and above the ways of human beings, and we accommodate our rationality within its narrow mechanistic strictures.

In putting forward these views, I recognise that I could be seen as offering another unchanging view of a world order to the one that I am seeking to replace. That is not my intention. I fully acknowledge that what I am considering here is my own conceptualisation of the nature of reality, and is my attempt to understand the forms of educational theory that our group is developing, both as forms by which we may understand our own reality, and as transformational forms which we feel mirror that reality. In this sense, I want to offer this book as a contribution to an educational theory that will dislodge the dominance of the linear order, both in terms of offering a view of unification as a recommended form for human living, and as an example of how that idea of unification may be seen as a form of human living.

In this I can imagine a scenario where, in the world of education—as much as it can be abstracted from its historical cultural context—the linear order is dissolved. Immediate implications would be: the 'front end' model of educational processes would disappear, and we would see education as a constantly evolving lifelong process that knew no barriers other than our own mortality; politically motivated departmentalisation would disappear, for people would recognise themselves and each other as people rather than schoolchildren, or students, or returners, or adult learners; line-management models for continuing professionalisation would disappear, for we would all be enquirers united in a common educational endeavour to improve the world; improvement would be effected through the open dialogue of compassionate individuals who are aiming to reach intersubjective understanding.

Such a view of wholeness is grounded in the idea of a generative order—that is, a form that is capable of reproducing itself infinitely through a limitless number of original creative transformations.

The form of the generative order is such that a base unit may be seen throughout the whole order in an enfolded or unfolded state (Bohm, 1983). Take, for example, the idea of the self-perpetuating action-reflection spiral that I put forward in 1984 and 1988. Here I suggested that the systematic problem-solving action plan as proposed by Whitehead may be seen as an open-ended procedure whereby questions latent within the enquirer's mind may be articulated as a systematic form of enquiry. Hence, the underlying question 'How do I improve my practice?' may be externalised in a coherent programme of action that shows a purposeful intent to improve a given situation. In Whitehead's formulation, this practical intent is given voice in the following (see also Chapter 3):

> I experience a problem when some of my educational values are
> denied in my practice;
> I imagine a solution to the problem;
> I act in the direction of the solution;
> I evaluate the solution;
> I modify my ideas and my actions in the light of the evaluation.

My own contribution has been to identify the idea of such a dialectical procedure as an example in practice of the notion of generative order. I offer a visualisation of my own conceptualisation as a spiral of spirals in which a 'base spiral' which, in this case, approximates to Whitehead's action plan

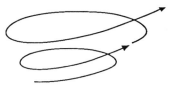

may transform itself infinitely to allow for creative episodes of practice, resulting in a form of enquiry that, although ordered, is not linear: hence:

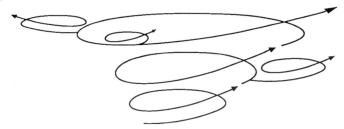

For me, the elegance of such generative order (and also its mind-stretching quality) is that it is seamless, with each part dissolving into the whole. For each notionally 'separate' spiral is in fact enfolded within the overall pattern, and itself has the potential to unfold in myriad forms, each form an original manifestation of its underlying potential. What may be seen as the beginning is in fact a continuation of something that went before, and each notional final state enfolds what is yet to be.

(As an aside: it is interesting, and not a little disappointing, that people have frequently commented on my work as offering a model, in the sense that it offers a prescriptive action plan. Perhaps this is yet another example of the general tendency to latch onto a familiar aspect of the linear order, and adapt an idea in order to accommodate it within the dominant tradition. I have never offered my work as a model, in the sense of the articulation of a procedure. What I am suggesting is that by adopting a world view of the wholeness and indivisibility of consciousness and its cultural-social manifestations, we liberate ourselves to entertain the idea of educational theory as transforming practice. If we entertain the notion of development as a continuum encompassing the whole field of human experience, and not an incremental series of accumulating singularities, it is not difficult to see the interplay of theory, research and practice as constituting a particular way of life. My 'spiral of spirals' is an attempt to capture the essence of this wholeness, an attempt to abstract in a notional form the idea of development as being an enfolding and an unfolding of an implicate order. It is not, and never has been, offered as a model, other than to suggest that a generative order is a model of reality that is more reflective of human enquiry and human experience in general than a linear order which reduces human experience to the common denominators of cause and effect.)

In terms of educational theory, we need to acknowledge that the currently dominant propositional form is inappropriate for helping us to understand the reality of a world view of the wholeness and indivisibility of consciousness. While we need to acknowledge the value of the propositional form and the incremental series of accumulating singularities which characterise most scientific and technical developments, we need to acknowledge also the notion of the generative order and its capacity to legitimate the art of the dialectician in holding both the one and the many together as a primal form of understanding. The whole notion of generative transformational order is one of coming into being, where the future and the past are contained within the ever-present now. Now is the ground for our endeavour. Now is the end of the beginning, and the beginning of the new: now is a different life-form from before, and has the capacity for the renewal of itself into an infinite number of transformed life-forms. Now is all that we have. Let us not waste it by trying to fit it in to an imagined linear order according to a constrained notion of where it should be; let us rather use it to let the meaning of our lives shine through, and enjoy it for what it is.

A summary of my own research project, then, is this:

I take the idea of generativity as the grounding of human enquiry. It is the base unit that holds within itself the potential for the realisation of an unlimited number of creative acts. Generative order may be seen as the process whereby transformations may be effected; and this notion may apply to enquiries concerning the evolution of consciousness and its social manifestation.

Generativity is a form of creative order that enables a thing to develop itself infinitely, by carrying out an unlimited number of self-transformations. In realising this capacity, a thing fulfils its own potential, thus contributing to the perpetuation of the good order of its own organic system. The process of self-realisation may be seen as a fundamental requirement of evolutionary processes.

Here are some examples of self-transforming systems that are grounded in the idea of generativity. (1) There are four basic rules of computation—adding, subtracting, multiplying and dividing—yet these four rules may transform themselves in such a way that they may realise their inherent potential to create an unlimited number of original computations. (2) Each human face is constituted of a limited number of physical components; yet the self-transformation of each component allows that an individual's face may never be replicated. (3) The finite rules of a language may generate an unlimited number of original utterances.

In my project I am trying to show how the idea of generative order may give us new perspectives on the constitution, the acquisition and the use of educational knowledge. I am trying to show how an individual's understanding of practice may be externalised through critical reflection, this understanding of the relationship between tacit and explicit itself constituting a form of educational knowledge. I take the acquisition of educational knowledge to be the development of understanding that rests in the dialectical process of question and answer, where each question has the generative capacity to transform itself into an answer, which in turn transforms into a form of question. The use of educational knowledge I take as the communication of individual understanding through dialogue, a highly moral enterprise that aims for personal action in the other's best interest.

In my view, when the idea of generative order is seen as the grounding of individual (and its transformed version, collaborative) critical reflection on social action, this gives rise to the establishment of the rule of freedom. By this I mean that a community may operate in a democratic fashion in that all members of that community freely agree the rules without coercion. They are brought together by their need to share a common concern about which they may hold different opinions. The rules give a form to the process of arriving at the agreement rather than impose a structure of conduct within a framework. In order to engage in the process, we have to share in a common vision that such a life is possible.

By drawing out the implications of the dynamic relationships that hold between the ideas of generative order and the transformational nature of educative relationships, I hope to realise my own sense of vision that the development of educational knowledge may encourage the evolution of a rational society. In doing so, I hope to support the notion of a form of educational theory with generative transformational capacity (Whitehead's idea of a 'living educational theory') that is grounded in the real conversations of people as they discuss with each other how they may realise their educational values in and through their practice, and how they may justify their claims to educational knowledge.

What I am trying to do in this part of the text is to demonstrate how I need to test these ideas against the reality of my own and other people's practice, to see if the ideas hold together. For if I am to live up to my own theory, I can no longer make claims on behalf of others according to my own understanding. I have to let other people speak for themselves.

Mary Is what you are talking about the voice FOR or the voice OF our community, Jack, because I think there's a difference.

Jack It's the voice OF our sense of community.

Mary Yes.

Jack As we were talking earlier about some of the anxieties you had about how you could make your own research more effective, now, I felt that was your voice, which, in relation to what you can be about both in collaborative action and your own individual action, would be your voice coming through. Now that would be FOR our community.

Mary   For, yes. There is a difference.

Jack   Oh, there is.

Mary   And the OF has to be a collaborative expression.

So here I am testing my own idea that educational enquiry is a generative transformational process. I am attempting to do this in the hermeneutic way, of offering excerpts from the conversation throughout the text, to illustrate the ideas; and also, over time, of offering the responses to the text of my colleagues.

I want to focus now on the idea of the need for self explanation as a fundamental aspect of action research, and to see again if I am living out my own values through the writing of this book.

Self explanation is a concept fundamental to educational enquiry. It contains the idea of generativity and self critique—that is, while I make claims about what is and what is not the case, can I demonstrate the foundation for those claims in and through my own life? This is something that not everyone does—indeed very few people do; and it is difficult to see how anyone who professes to be engaged in educational enquiry can call what they are doing 'educational' when they are not prepared to show what they mean by that—that is, what significance the research in which they are engaged has for their own lives.

Allan Bloom has made just this point in 'The Closing of the American Mind' (1987, pp. 203-204). Nietzsche, says Bloom, recognised that he was inevitably influenced by the heritage of his own culture.

"It is Nietzsche's merit that he was aware that to philosophize is radically problematic in the cultural, historicist dispensation. He recognized the terrible intellectual and moral risks involved. At the centre of his every thought was the question 'How is it possible to do what I am doing?' He tried to apply to his own thought the teachings of cultural relativism. This practically nobody else does. For example,

Freud says that men are motivated by desire for sex and power, but he did not apply those motives to explain his own science or his own scientific activity. But if he can be a true scientist, i.e. motivated by love of the truth, so can other men, and his description of their motives is thus mortally flawed. Or if he is motivated by sex or power, he is not a scientist, and his science is only one means among many possible to attain those ends. This contradiction runs right throughout the natural and social sciences. They give an account of things that cannot possibly explain the conduct of their practitioners. The highly ethical economist who speaks only about gain, the public-spirited political scientist who sees only group interest, the physicist who signs petitions in favour of freedom while recognizing only unfreedom ... are symptomatic of the difficulty of providing a self-explanation for science and a ground for the theoretical life, which has dogged the mind since early modernity but has become particularly acute with cultural relativism."

(Bloom, 1987)

I am saying that, as educators, we need to submit our own practice to the scrutiny of others, to see if we are indeed engaging in our own self-explanation. Does our community of researchers at Bath do this? I think we do.

Jean   After Moira and Jack and I had that original conversation which now appears as Part One of this text, I went away and transcribed the tapescript. We had already talked about the possibility of taping the conversation and linking it with the first draft that I had already sent in. So I re-jigged the text in terms of a dual text—an outer and an inner text. The outer text was actually constituted by the conversation that we had already had and pointed out the need for producing manuscripts that talk about the necessity of producing accounts of our own practice, but it also demonstrated the living reality of how our practice evolved. The outer text then of the dialogue actually demonstrated what the inner text was suggesting. I like to think that there is now quite a nice integrity between the theory and the practice, that a relationship flows through the two texts. Do you think that that has actually worked, Jack?

Jack   I think it's worked in the sense of people engaging with each other's ideas and showing how dialogue can help you to move forward, in both understanding and action. It is for me something which has got the potential to become a living and dynamic form and which can hold the development of the community within its representation, so you can now be showing what the development of our community really does look like. That would be for me the voices here trying to explain what it is that individually and collectively we're trying to do to move forward in terms of the increasing power that you get in the sense of belonging to a community. So you get situations where we're all feeling under pressure. There's so much happening that denies the fundamental values that we came into education to live out, and yet when we're together today, when we try to talk through what it is we're trying to do, there's an alternative base, an alternative set of qualities, and I think that then enables us to say what we're going to be doing, to make our contribution, but we no longer feel isolated. We actually feel it is part of a community, and that strengthens us. So that is what I see as the power of what you're doing.

Later in the conversation:

Mary   You know, I find this quite difficult because a loosely formed group such as ourselves comes together and has such a strong sharing of values, or rather a sharing of very strong values, yet the nature of the community is so complex. It means different things to each one of us. I keep asking, 'What does it mean to belong to the Bath action research group?'

Jack   My worry is you may destroy by almost asking that kind of question. Now, the reason for saying this is that I think strength comes from shared action, respect for each other's action—and I like the way that you put it when you saw the shift from the idea of shared values to the expression of how we've learnt to share together the expression of strong values. But we know that we differ. We've learnt, I think, how to hold that sharing of strong values in the way that Alasdair MacIntyre recommends—he says that a university should have this function of learning how to contain in dialogue and productive work the expression of strong values while we may differ. I would have thought that is what we could actually focus on rather than almost the meaning.

Mary   Yes, but if you don't look at yourself critically as a community, then you may actually not be developing as a community, and I have that sense in which there is something very circular and repetitive about my involvement with this community which has offered me tremendous support over the last eight years; and yet as a psychologist I understand that unless you look at those interactional qualities you won't be able to develop, unless we can look at how we interact, what that means to our own personal growth, we will not actually grow as a community. I'm not sure how we do that.

Jean   Maybe we need to broaden our scope of action.

Mary   I think we just need to ask that question to start with. I mean the question of what this group means to each one of us and how we take from the group and how we interact and so on. What the community is about.

Jean   Are you articulating some sort of intent here, Mary? By saying this is something that we ought to look at as our group agenda if we are to go forward as a group?

Mary   I would say so, yes.

The questions I now need to ask colleagues are these:

How can we express our practical intention about improving our practice in the name of education and our own humanity, in a dialogical form, in a way which will enable us to judge our effectiveness?

Does this text embody a developing critical understanding of our educational development in our enquiries of the form 'How do I improve. . .?' Can we point to this developing understanding through our interaction with the text? And in that sense, have I fulfilled my purpose of trying to find a form, in allowing the text to evolve as it did, in which such critical understanding may be expressed?

I also need to ask you, the reader, to move the ideas forward within the dimensions of your own life. What are the values by which you judge your life? What is your practical intent in trying to live out those values? Do you think you can improve the world, and, if so, how? Please take time to write down your thoughts, and reflect on them, and see if the dialogues that we have recorded here involve you, so that you are moved to take part.

I will ask my colleagues to respond to my questions over time, to see how they are living our their values through their intentional actions. Part of my own programme of taking our community development forward will then be to reproduce those answers in the form of new manuscripts, which I hope, as a publisher, to encourage them to write, individually and collectively. I would also welcome responses from you, the reader, to see how we might further the idea of educational communities through producing books and texts which will show the process in action. This is my intention, as part of the values that I hold as an educator, of offering in public the demonstration of that view of the indivisibility of human endeavour to make the world a happier place.

Chapter Seven

Generativity and Educational Discourse

I think it is very difficult for most of us to appreciate what free dialogue is, and even more difficult to handle it. It is quite threatening to be faced with the responsibility of stating my own view instead of responding to someone else's. Yet this, I feel, is what is a characteristic of dialogue that is free and is conducive to the continuing development of the participants - accepting the responsibility of interpreting the world from my own point of view (Polanyi, 1958) and making a commitment to that knowledge with the intent of helping others to see its relevance in my life—and their own, if they wish.

These feelings were articulated by our community:

Mary   It's difficult to belong to this group, in that we are an egalitarian group, aren't we? In the sense that we haven't got a traditional structure of a committee where you've got to have a president, a secretary, a treasurer, a washer-upper, a convener ... and most people do want to participate. I do worry actually that to participate in this group is not always easy. There are those who have a lot to say, and those who haven't. I worry that some of us seem to dominate, not through the force of our argument, but through the force of our personality.

Peter   Yes. It's one thing to make quick statements in support of another person's arguments. It's another thing to ask questions yourself. I feel this quite distinctly as part of my experience. I feel that I am legitimised in shoving in a quick one-liner in the hopes that it helps me, and possibly somebody else. But actually to pose a question is another thing, because that can halt the whole conversation in its tracks if it's the wrong question. It is awesome for me to ask a question and believe as I ask it that people are going to be prepared to stop and answer it. Which is part of the dialectic. You can't progress without asking questions. But it's a higher-order thing in terms of courage. So far as I can see, making a big statement to reinforce somebody else's point is all right; asking a question of your own is something of a different order entirely.

Mary   That reluctance—you've described exactly the way in which I feel I belong to one of the committees on which I serve! It's the fact here that all members actually feel that they can contribute, and that's a particularly significant issue, isn't it. There are strong feelings in this community, and I say that with great respect, and we all feel entitled to contribute.

Engaging in this kind of free dialogue is challenging, because it means that I have to face the fact that I am a social being and I must be prepared to change as necessary. By this I mean that I live with others—I always have done—and inevitably I have been fashioned to a certain extent by my circumstances—that is, the conditions of my upbringing, the people with whom I have been in contact, the whole socio-economic structure of which I am a part. I have developed my own infrastructure of prejudices and assumptions. So have the people with whom I am in contact. We might not fully realise it, but we are, each and every one of us, to a great extent the product of each other's consciousness. Although we say that we are independent, socially, intellectually and culturally, we have to acknowledge that our independence is enfolded within, and itself is conditioned by, our society with others.

As a result, we hold, individually and collectively, a host of assumptions and prejudices—those of the indiosyncratic kind of individuals (I don't like people who wear green hats, for example), and those of the normative kind (we don't like people who jump queues). Our whole society has its being in prejudice and assumption of one kind or another: we have our givens, our taken-for-granteds, that restrict our individual and collective consciousness within a rigid infrastructure. It would be monumentally difficult to engage in a form of discourse that defies the rules of the infrastructure and dislodges the foundations.

Why? Because it means that not only I, but also my companions, have to accept that we need to step out of the framework, and suspend judgement. We need to suspend judgement both about the character of the framework we have just left, and about the new ideas we are about to encounter. It is difficult enough for me to do this as a person alone who has decided to take this step. How much more unlikely would it be to be a part of a scenario where several of us did it.

Yet I think this is what our community at Bath is aiming to do.

Kevin   I found it really a kind of fundamental statement when we were talking this morning, when Erica said, 'Let's make the focus of our conference in March the way that people feel shot at by those in power.' And it's a way of giving power back to teaching—making teachers aware of their sense of community and the strength that they can draw from each other in groups like this. And it's at that point that this feeling of community and mutual support dives back into practice and into action because of that feeling that we've got; we can now think of offering other people who may wish to have the same kind of support the potential for developing their own networks. So that kind of link between the feeling we've got here and actual concrete action is the same. That's the value of what we're doing as a self-reflective community.

Jean   Have I got this right? You're saying that we're a group of practitioners who share very strong values, who trust each other. We meet here voluntarily because we each get out of it what we need, we take away with us what we need to take out of the group, but our intent as a group is to share with others who want to listen. We can show the real benefits that our being together has brought to us, so that they can take that on as well. We're saying that we are not dependent on the power structures that were already in existence. We're generating our own knowledge base.

Kevin   We're not dominating each other.

Jean   Right. We have worked out a democratic community for ourselves and we are looking possibly to making that sense of community public, so that other people can see that it actually is possible.

Mary   It's better than a self-help group, though, isn't it? That's what that sounded like.

Peter   It sounded a bit like the early Christian martyrs getting together.

Mary   I can identify with that. In a sense there is a mission.

Jean   I think there's a very strong sense of mission, only possibly we've never articulated it in those terms.

Moira   It is a sense of being empowered as a source of inspiration for the aridity of our professional lives.

Kevin   Say that again, Moira. It sounded really good.

Moira   I think it does offer some sort of inspiration to combat against the aridity of some of the rest of our professional lives. It's that arid nature of what some of us do. For example, when Jack's not here I feel isolated. When Jack's here, he and I can have conversations which actually send me away feeling, 'Yes, there is someone who not necessarily shares every value that I hold but someone who will listen to the values that I hold and who will want to see them in operation. So it's important to me to be in a community in which I feel that, as Mary said, I can share some of my very strongly held values, that they will be listened to, that they can be challenged, within a situation that is not draining of my energy, my professional commitment, but actually enhances that professional commitment—a kind of shared tolerance. That's very important.

Phil   A sense of affirmation—that's important. Criticise someone's ideas, and still affirm their importance, whereas most of what we get is criticism which actually denies our right to hold the values that we do.

Moira   What I am saying is that unless we feel secure that we have both the right and the insight which we accrue from the community to affect our practice for the sake of improvement, then we are never going to get to any kind of theory, anyway.

Phil   Yes. Because at the end of the day all this is going to be going into classrooms and the kids are going to be on the receiving end of it. The sense of community, as you were saying, must be there because that's the whole point, almost.

Jean   The living theory.

Moira   Yes.

Jean   Are we rejecting the dominance of abstracted theory?

Moira   I am. I don't know whether we are, but I am.

Jean   We have this as a living educational community, and we are generating a new kind of theory.

I think the difficulties inherent in the idea of free dialogue are compounded when the discussion is to do with the nature of knowledge. Here is the need for critique. Here we have a clear demonstration of the need to turn a thing back on itself in order to examine its own constitution. For in this instance we are considering how knowledge may be used to examine the idea of knowledge. How difficult it is to suspend judgement about what constitutes a legitimate form of knowledge in order to entertain a proposal that there are other, equally legitimate forms of knowledge. That suspension of judgement has to be effected by a knower who is confident enough in her own sense of self to suspend her own prejudices and listen to another with compassion and interest, with the conscious intent of changing her mind, if faced with a better argument.

I think this is what our community is working towards. We engage in creative dialogue by respecting ourselves and the others as equal, as worthy of regard. We do not dominate. We do not acknowledge any form of externally imposed power structures. Rather, we delight in the fact that each individual is legitimated in creating his or her individual knowledge, and to share it. This process of sharing is the source of the power. This is generativity at work—where I create my own knowledge which in turn transforms into you creating your knowledge, and the transition phases whereby my knowledge becomes yours pass over almost unnoticed as we transform one into the other. Knowledge itself transforms into better versions of itself, and knowers transform themselves as well—as individuals and as communities.

Our community has grown in this sense. We all acknowledge the fact that Jack brought us together in the first place, as supervisor of our studies. But many of us have left the university as such: we have completed our formal programme of study. Yet, in my view, we constitute a group that can offer a new form of educational and scholarly communication which is a realisation of some of the values expressed by MacIntyre (1990): that a university community should be one in which knowledge is generated through critical and supportive dialogue.

Jack   The last Vice Chancellor, in 1981, was on the University Council, and he was talking about the function of a university. He said active researchers should be thinking now about the significance of their work for the next century, because a university, if it's anything, should provide illumination, and, largely through the accumulated works in the university library, should be that resource for use by the community which acts like a civilising influence on that community. Now, if we think of this idea that Jean is producing a text which I would be very happy with if it would just allow us to feel a shared sense of community. So when we think of a wider audience it seems to be a form of representing what we do together which we can identify with and feel that incredible sense of satisfaction of just belonging together because it's here. It's rather like Peggy Kok with her M.Ed.. I read that last chapter, and because it is so intensely to do with my relationship with her, all the transcript data, it means a lot to me. I identify with that. If Jean could do something similar for us, so that our voices were coming through, I'd feel very happy with that. We could then do what Terry, I think, is advocating, which is to find a way of editing in order to communicate to a wider audience. At least we would have ourselves the satisfaction of feeling yes, this really is as we believe it to be.

Later in the conversation:

Jack   The library is full of traditional kinds of text. Where is the idea that a university ought to be doing what we've been doing today? Alasdair MacIntyre advocates that what we've been doing, and exactly what Moira and Mary have been saying, should be the base of a university community. Now, what I think we ought to be trying to achieve is a form of communication of the kind that we're having today but which is presented through Jean's power of writing, so we recognise each other in what Jean writes. She will use our voices from here. That is, if it can be moved into the university context and celebrated as a form of understanding which is a living and organic form of understanding; so it's always in relation not necessarily only to ourselves, but also to what others are doing in their professional lives and being reflected within what counts as knowledge within the university. A living educational form—that is what I'm after. I'm after a university that actually celebrates, as knowledge, as forms of understanding, what we've actually been talking about. I think there's something quite new emerging out of this kind of conversation, if Jean can find the form to present it, because I can see how it can develop on an individual basis, as we demonstrate here, through questions of the kind 'How do I improve what I'm doing?', and collectively—but that's what Moira said about the 'we'—she's always nervous about using 'we'.

Moira   I'm very sensitive to the fact that Jack will not use 'we' except in specific instances in which he's defined the parameters of 'we'.

Jack   So I can use it here, the first time in relation to 'we'. I can use it in terms of what's been said today. I can use 'we' and feel very committed and affirming.

Jean   One implication would be that next year when this text has become part of the library stock and people are reading it within the School of Education, that there will be half a dozen of these groups operating.

Jack   That would be good. I'd be delighted if we could communicate.

Mary   I have some tensions about this group being centred in the university. I would have that same vision about how a university should be—perhaps an idealistic view—and I'm very happy for this group to be based here, but I don't see our function as being university-based.

Jack   Alasdair MacIntyre is talking about re-conceiving the university and the lecture so it's in a sense of a process of reconstruction. Our contribution could be undermined and distorted if we thought we were just putting it into an existing structure.

Phil   The existing structure does exist, and the idea that you were talking about is an idea.

Jack   It's more than that. I think with all the action research texts—the PhDs, the MPhils, that are now in the university library—I felt that this was part of this process of transforming what we hoped we would be able to achieve into what we can actually show that we have achieved.

In the next chapter I shall pick up this point of how texts may exist as the evidence of the generative order, and actually contribute to bringing about the reconstruction of the idea of an educational community, in that educational theory is located in living, dialogical forms of communication which demonstrate its own evolution, rather than in the reified forms of propositional discourse.

Here, I have to say that I share Mary's view that, because the group meets at the university, it might be seen as a university-based group. I think this is true to a certain extent, and I think that if, by virtue of the fact that we are part of the university, we can effect some reform, some re-conceptualisation of the idea of what it means to belong to a university, and the function of a university, then our presence there is justified.

I think, however, that this is part of a wider issue, and one that I have been articulating throughout the text. I think action research is a form of enquiry that is not exclusive to academics, or, indeed, to professional teachers. I think it is a vehicle for all of us who feel that we have a contribution to make, and are determined to explore the nature of that contribution as it effects change in our own lives before we consciously try to effect change in others. I think we are all potentially teachers, provided we accept that we are learners, too, for teaching and learning are two sides of the same coin, transforming and transforming again as part of the generative enterprise.

I have to say (and I know that this view is not shared by all my colleagues in the group, though it is by some) that I see clear parallels between my professional life as a teacher, and my spiritual life as a Christian. In fact, for me, the two previously separate strands of my life have now integrated, and I draw no clear distinction between them. My spiritual life is the grounding for everything that I do. I draw strength and inspiration from visits to Church, and my communication with others who share the same values and beliefs, and this inspiration fires me to engage in purposeful action, even when I don't feel like it. The same principles apply to my life with other action researchers. In response to Mary's question, 'What does it mean to me to be a member of the Bath action research group?', it means that I am able to check with the others where I have come from and where I am, and draw strength from them to know more clearly where I am going.

Chapter Eight

Generating the Evidence

I have been working as a writer for nearly ten years, and throughout this time I have become increasingly aware of the paradox of trying to present living forms of thought through non-living print—an organic message through an inorganic medium; and this awareness has caused me to focus seriously on the problem of the ambiguity of written material.

Phil   It's squaring that notion about a living educational theory and producing work that for a section of the community is not in tune with the idea. I have difficulty in my own mind of putting together the idea of the dialectic of the living community with this notion that somehow dialectic comes to an end with producing the evidence for the future.

I have followed this problem through systematically in my project, of how a text can be at one and the same time the vehicle for working out ideas (1989), the manifestation in action of latent ideas (1990), an expression of intent and instrument of critique (1992), and its own evidence of the ideas it is putting forward (this book). In this, I think the form of this text is unusual, though not original (see, for example, Bohm, 1987), and therefore probably needs more intellectual effort on the part of the reader than straightforward 'traditional' texts that present ideas on a 'take it or leave it' basis. Here I am asking you to work with me, really to try to get inside the text and work from inside out, rather than see the book only as existing within your outside-in perception of things in space and time. This is a problem which was felt also by my companions, the problem of presenting an unfamiliar form to a general readership.

Kevin   When you wrote the first part, did you keep a sense of time-line in there, because in a view of dialectical knowledge, it's the development of something over a period of time, and if you are reflecting, it might be worth asking, are you dating the conversations, the transcripts—'This is what we said at this particular time about this particular text here that I am writing now'.

Jean   I have dated what I put in as a prologue which was an extract from that conversation, yes.

Kevin   I think trying to establish what was talked about, and what was said about what, when, is part of the process of capturing in an honest manner the real dialectical development that goes on through time. That time-line is very important in our idea of dialectic.

Moira   I think you characterise that by the phrase your 'best thinking to date'. You keep using that through the text.

Jean   Yes.

Kevin   The second question is this question of audience. One of the doubts that I have about my own writing in trying to capture this dialectical development over time—How does someone react to that? Would they want to follow the story through? Or would they feel more comfortable with a different form, presentation? I remember I was asked by someone at a BERA conference in 1985 about a paper I had given. He said, 'I've just read your paper. I found the whole presentation completely foreign to me.' That's always stuck with me. There are people out there who will find this way of communicating difficult to handle. I don't know how important that is.

Terry   I think you write in different ways for different audiences. There's nothing wrong with taking a set piece which you feel happy with and feel you will communicate quite happily with the majority of the audience that you're wanting to reach, and then saying, 'I will re-work that, make it accessible to a different audience'. We did that with our County journal. What we did was to take pieces that were submitted, that had been written for a particular purpose, and sub-edited them to make them more accessible to a more general readership. I think that we very seldom just write one piece. I think very often we write twice.

In this text particularly I want to focus on the idea of capturing the evidence of living, evolving systems (including living communities) through a form that is in itself static (printed matter). I think that this in fact is an example of the generative capacity within evolving systems. Let's say my ideas develop quite rapidly, but, in order to let the ideas become well-formed over time through actually filtering them out into my actions in the world, noting how they take on meaning in and through my life, I have to go through interchanging periods of action and reflection. Every now and again I have to synthesise. I have to analyse my action and my reflection on my evolving ideas, and I have to consolidate my thinking in some form or another so that I can go forward from my position of review into a new phase of action and reflection. For me personally the best form of consolidation is to write it down. I have engaged in my own action-reflection in order to raise tacit ideas at competence into an active way of life realised at performance (McNiff, 1990). This strategy does not suit everyone. Clearly it does not suit dyslexics, nor other people who have trouble with words, oral or written. (I have recently started exploring with a friend who has problems with written words how she synthesises the symbols she uses in her reasoning. In my own thinking, my first-order symbolic form of representation is colours, shapes and patterns; words are a kind of second-order analogue of primary visual images.)

Whatever strategy we might adopt, however, it seems sensible to think that periods of analysis may be consolidated with periods of synthesis, albeit in a notional form; and within some strategies (such as producing texts) these synthesising periods may be seen as critical transition junctures. A text itself may be seen as existing at a transition point.

This text certainly does. It exists as a summative expression of my thinking to date, and the testing out of some of my more recent ideas against those of my colleagues. Colleagues in the community have expressed some views about the nature of the group and their sense of mission, which now have to be tested out against the wider community.

I am offering the text as evidence of the parallel processes of the growth of people's understanding and the growth of communication processes—the first through the recorded conversations of the participants, and the second through the process of writing the text.

Terry picked up this idea within our conversation:

Terry   You said the text had evolved, Jean. Let me ask you something about that evolutionary process. You were saying that you transcribed the taped conversation between yourself, Moira and Jack.

Jean   Yes.

Terry   I guessed you did. It would be interesting some time, possibly, to explore what happens to your perception of the original text in the light not only of our conversation but of the actual process of transcribing the conversation, because I'm very well aware of the fact that when I'm actually writing something, something different does happen. I would guess that in the process, because you transcribe it yourself, rather than sub-contracting the transcription, that there may well be something that happens in your thought processes that actually helps the final text to emerge in the form that it does.

Moira   Also those aspects from the transcript that you choose to integrate within the text—that is something that you have done without consultation with Jack and me, for example.

Jean   But I have put the text back to you, to say, 'Do you approve?'

Moira   I'm not making a judgemental point. I'm saying that's also a part of the process that might be hidden.

Terry   That is the process, isn't it. It's that process of the actual thought processes that go on during your transcription bit and also the way in which you edit that— and it needs editing—what effect that has on the final text.

Peter   But whatever your processes are, surely the thing that matters at the end as far as I can see is that for an ordinary reader out there, there is no smell of artifice. Otherwise they could simply say, 'You've taken all this great wealth of words and picked and chosen to back up what you had in mind as your hypothesis in the first place'.

So I am saying in this chapter that a book may be a living element within the dynamic process of dialectical development. The ideas which have been enfolded within my mind have been transformed into living reality through a dialogue of encouragement with my companions. The book that is the manifest expression of those ideas is enfolded within our future lives—will unfold over time in and through our lives, and through the lives of its readers, if and when they see the relevance to their own lives and decide to apply it there. It is only through time and honest endeavour that we shall discover if in fact it has meaning to a community outside that of its creators.

Phil   In trying to capture the essence of what we are doing, there is a sense in which we could destroy the thing which uniquely characterises the kind of work and the kind of sense of community you are talking about. As soon as it's put into the form of books and so on, it's just on shelves, then it becomes like anything else at the university. I'm not trying to labour this, but I think there's a real dilemma involved. This is what Erica and Kevin were saying earlier about how sensitive do we need to be about communicating this to an outside audience? Those kinds of issues. When we're actually talking here, now, that's where the dialectic is as far as I'm concerned. It's in the nature of the conversation and the sense of community. It's when we're together, communing together. As soon as that takes forms which are part of pre-existing organisations within the university, then I begin to worry that we might actually begin to lose the core of the very thing that makes what we do unique.

Jack   I share that unease.

Kevin   I don't. I've shared how you all feel at times, but it's dangerous to let it take too high a priority in your thinking. To give an example: I've worried for a long time about the fact that I've found writers like J. Britton and N. Martin valuable in my own teaching, even though the form of their writing is very much a propositional form. Both were part of a conventional sort of university-based academic writing about English teaching. What I was trying to do in my writing was to show what English teaching actually looks like and to form a theory from practice in that kind of way. I thought, 'Am I being corrupted by taking on what J. Britton says?' I think the answer is 'No, I'm not'. What I'm doing is engaging in a dialogue with, if you like, provisional propositions that he is making. I am taking on what he's saying, adapting it to my own situation and transmuting it as I'm doing so. So there's a very dynamic process going on. And if, for example, publications came out of this community of ours, I think that they will themselves be used, transmuted, in further dialectical processes.

Phil   When Jack talks about the implications of our work for the next century ... if we're writing, and we share each other's work, and we share the work of others, and we discuss it, then this becomes part of the present community because we share it. But I'm conscious that there's a point at which it ceases only to be part of the present and becomes a catalyst for the future.

Peter   Don't you make another turn of the hermeneutic circle? As time goes by you're looking at the artefact, as it were from a greater distance, culturally and temporally, and so you just have to bring out bigger hermeneutic guns, so to speak, in terms of your own response to it.

Jack   Why isn't it possible to think that there are certain acts of creation which other people do like to come back to and recognise as part of the very important process of your own genesis ...

Kevin   *If you engage in living forms, that's never actually lost because it becomes part of somebody else's consciousness and then that in turn becomes part of somebody else's consciousness and at some point in the future—ten, fifteen years— people may, should they wish to do so, track back that kind of genealogical line of what they're doing, the kinds of things they're working on, the values that they hold, the things that they're trying to get across, back to groups like this one and the action research movement over the 1980s and early 1990s. So it matters that it's a live performance because it's communicating and what is done through live performance, even though it may not be written down in the form of a text, still has an effect.*

Phil   *I'll share that. I'm conscious that I'm in danger of creating an emphasis here, but I do think there's a distinction here that's quite important in the essence of what we're trying to do. There is a real danger that we lose our spontaneity in concentrating on the forms in which we are trying to express it.*

Jack   *That only becomes important, if you like, if in making your contribution public in a particular form you distort it beyond recognition, so that it's no longer serving a useful purpose. We'll only find out by Jean trying to reconstruct a work and then trying it out, first amongst ourselves and see does this really work, is it something we can identify with, and then trying with others to see if it works there.*

Phil   *It's part of the action enquiry process.*

Bibliography

Adelman, C., 'The Practical Ethic takes Priority over Methodology', in Carr, W., QUALITY IN TEACHING (Falmer, 1989).

Altrichter, H., Kemmis, S., McTaggart, R., and Zuber-Skerritt, O., 'Defining, confining or refining action research?' in Zuber-Skerritt, O. (ed), ACTION RESEARCH FOR CHANGE AND DEVELOPMENT (Avebury, Gower Publishing Company Limited, 1991).

Avon Local Education Authority: YOU AND YOUR PROFESSIONAL DEVELOPMENT (Avon Local Education Authority).

Bernstein, R., BEYOND OBJECTIVITY AND RELATIVITY; SCIENCE, HERMENEUTICS AND PRAXIS (Basil Blackwell, 1983).

Bernstein, R., THE NEW CONSTELLATION (Polity Press, 1991).

Bohm, D., WHOLENESS AND THE IMPLICATE ORDER (Ark Paperbacks, 1983).

Bohm, D., UNFOLDING MEANING (Ark Paperbacks, 1987).

Bohm, D. and Peat, F.D., SCIENCE, ORDER AND CREATIVITY (Routledge, 1989).

Bloom, A., THE CLOSING OF THE AMERICAN MIND (Wiley, 1987).

Brookfield, S.D., DEVELOPING CRITICAL THINKERS (Open University Press, 1987).

Buber, M., BETWEEN MAN AND MAN (Fontana, 1947).

Buber, M., THE KNOWLEDGE OF MAN (Allen and Unwin, 1965).

Carr, W. and Kemmis, S., BECOMING CRITICAL: EDUCATION, KNOWLEDGE AND ACTION RESEARCH (Falmer Press, 1986).

Chomsky, N., ASPECTS OF THE THEORY OF SYNTAX (MIT, 1965).

Chomsky, N., KNOWLEDGE OF LANGUAGE: ITS NATURE, ORIGIN AND USE (Praeger Publishers, 1986).

Collingwood, R.G., AN AUTOBIOGRAPHY (Oxford University Press, 1939).

Day, C., 'Professional Development and Change in the 1990s; Issues for Action

Researchers': (Opening address presented at the Classroom Action Research Network International Conference, University of Nottingham, 1991).

Eames, K., *'Growing Your Own'*, British Journal of In-Service Education,Vol.16, No.2, Autumn (1990); also in McNiff, J., TEACHING AS LEARNING: AN ACTION RESEARCH APPROACH (Routledge, 1992).

Ebbutt, D., *'Educational Action Research: Some General Concerns and Specific Quibbles'* mimeo (Cambridge Institute of Education, 1982).

Elliott, J., *'Action Research: Framework for Self Evaluation in Schools'*, TIQL Working Paper, No. 1, mimeo (Cambridge Institute of Education, 1981).

Elliott, J., *'Educational Theory and the Professional Learning of Teachers: an overview'* in Cambridge Journal of Education, Vol. 19, No. 1 (1989).

Elliott, J., ACTION RESEARCH FOR EDUCATIONAL CHANGE (Open University Press, 1991).

Grene, M., THE KNOWER AND THE KNOWN (Faber and Faber, 1966).

Habermas, J., KNOWLEDGE AND HUMAN INTERESTS (trans. J.J. Shapiro) (Heinemann, 1972).

Habermas, J., COMMUNICATION AND THE EVOLUTION OF SOCIETY (Trans. T. McCarthy) (Heinemann, 1979).

Habermas, J., THE THEORY OF COMMUNICATIVE ACTION, VOLUME TWO: THE CRITIQUE OF FUNCTIONALIST REASON (Trans. T. McCarthy) (Basil Blackwell, 1981).

Kemmis, S. and McTaggart, R., THE ACTION RESEARCH PLANNER (Geelong, Victoria, University Press, 1982).

Kok, P., THE ART OF AN EDUCATIONAL ENQUIRER (unpub. M.Ed. dissertation, University of Bath, 1991).

Larter, A., AN ACTION RESEARCH APPROACH TO CLASSROOM DISCUSSION IN THE EXAMINATION YEARS (Unpub. MPhil. dissertation, University of Bath, 1987).

Lewin, K., *'Action Research and Minority Problems'*, Journal of Social Sciences, Vol. 2 (1946).

Lomax, P. (ed), THE MANAGEMENT OF CHANGE: BERA DIALOGUES NUMBER 1 (Multilingual Matters, 1989).

Lomax, P., MANAGING BETTER SCHOOLS AND COLLEGES: AN ACTION RESEARCH WAY: BERA DIALOGUES NUMBER 5 (Multilingual Matters, 1991).

MacIntyre, A., AFTER VIRTUE: A STUDY IN MORAL THEORY (Duckworth, London, 1981).

MacIntyre, A., THREE RIVAL VERSIONS OF MORAL ENQUIRY: ENCYCLOPAEDIA, GENEALOGY, AND TRADITION: BEING GIFFORD LECTURES DELIVERED IN THE UNIVERSITY OF EDINBURGH IN 1988 (Duckworth, 1990).

McNiff, J., *'Action Research: A Generative Model for In-Service Support'*, British

Journal of In-Service Education, Vol. 10, No. 3, Summer (1984).

McNiff, J., ACTION RESEARCH: PRINCIPLES AND PRACTICE (Macmillan Education, 1988).

McNiff, J., *'Writing and the Creation of Educational Knowledge'* in Lomax, P. (ed), MANAGING STAFF DEVELOPMENT IN SCHOOLS: AN ACTION RESEARCH APPROACH: BERA DIALOGUES NUMBER 3 (Multilingual Matters, 1990).

McNiff, J., *'An Individual's Claim to Understand Her Own Educational Development'* in Ryan, C. (ed), PROCESSES OF REFLECTION AND ACTION (Classroom Action Research Network Publication 10B, 1991).

McNiff, J., TEACHING AS LEARNING: AN ACTION RESEARCH APPROACH (forthcoming, Routledge, 1992).

Polanyi, M., PERSONAL KNOWLEDGE (Routledge and Kegan Paul, 1958).

Polanyi, M., KNOWING AND BEING (Routledge and Kegan Paul, 1969).

Polanyi, M., *'Understanding Ourselves'* in Ornstein, R. (ed), THE NATURE OF HUMAN CONSCIOUSNESS (San Francisco; W.R. Freeman and Co., 1973).

Popper, K., OBJECTIVE KNOWLEDGE (Oxford University Press, 1972).

Rudduck, J., *'The Language of Consciousness and the Landscape of Action'* in British Educational Research Journal, Vol.17, No.4 (1991).

Ryle, G., THE CONCEPT OF MIND (Harmondsworth: Penguin, 1949).

Stenhouse, L., INTRODUCTION TO CURRICULUM RESEARCH AND DEVELOPMENT (Heinemann Education, 1975).

Stenhouse, L., *'Research is Systematic Enquiry Made Public'* in British Educational Research Journal 9(1) 11-20 (1983).

Sternberg, R.J., WISDOM: ITS NATURE, ORIGINS AND DEVELOPMENT (Cambridge University Press, 1990).

Tillich, P., THE COURAGE TO BE (Collins: Fount Paperbacks, 1977).

Torbert, W., *'Why Has Educational Research Been So Uneducational?'* in Reason, P. and Rowan, J. (eds), HUMAN INQUIRY (Wiley, 1981).

Whitehead, J., *'The Use of Personal Educational Theories in In-Service Education'* in British Journal of In-Service Education, Vol.9, No.3, (1983).

Whitehead, J., *'An Analysis of an Individual's Educational Development: the Basis for Personally Oriented Action Research'* in Shipman, M. (ed), EDUCATIONAL RESEARCH: PRINCIPLES, POLICIES AND PRACTICES (Falmer Press, 1985).

Whitehead, J., *'How do we Improve Research-based Professionalism in Education?— A question which includes action research, educational theory and the politics of educational knowledge'* in British Journal of In-Service Education, Vol.15, No.1 (1989a).

Whitehead, J., *'Creating a Living Educational Theory from Questions of the*

Kind, "How do I Improve my Practice?"' in Cambridge Journal of Education, Vol.19, No.1 (1989b).

Whitehead, J., *'How do I improve my professional practice as an academic and educational manager?'* A paper presented to the First World Congress on Action Research and Process Management, Brisbane (1990).

Whitehead, J., *'How can my Philosophy of Action Research Transform and Improve my Professional Practice and Produce a Good Social Order?'*—A Response to Ortrun Zuber-Skerritt (Second World Congress on Action Learning, 1992).

Winter, R., LEARNING FROM EXPERIENCE (Falmer Press, 1989).

Zuber-Skerritt, O. (ed), ACTION RESEARCH FOR CHANGE AND DEVELOPMENT, Avebury (1991a).

Zuber-Skerritt, O., PROFESSIONAL DEVELOPMENT IN HIGHER EDUCATION: A THEORETICAL FRAMEWORK FOR ACTION RESEARCH (Griffith University, Brisbane, 1991b).

Index